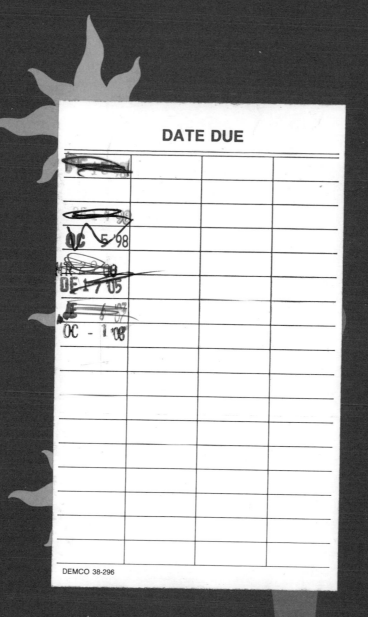

MOBILE
୭ m a g i c ୭

MOBILE

magic

Innovative ideas for airborne accessories

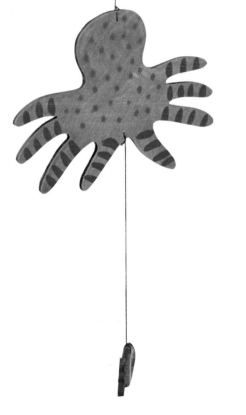

Over 80 creations and inspirations

Juliet Bawden

Special photography by
Lucy Mason

LORENZ BOOKS

NEW YORK • LONDON • SYDNEY • BATH

Publisher's note

When making mobiles for babies and young children there are some special points
that must be remembered for safety. Use natural fabrics, such as wool, cotton or felt, wherever
possible. Choose non-toxic decorating materials, especially paints, glues and varnishes.
Only use non-toxic flame-retardant polyester wadding for padding. Any mobile with small pieces or
containing wire should not be handled by babies or suspended directly above a baby's cot or carriage.
Decorations, however firmly attached, can be expertly dismantled by little fingers and
are a potential hazard. Attach such a mobile out of reach and to one side of wherever the baby
is sitting or lying, so she or he can look at it and enjoy its shape, color and
the movements it makes in perfect safety.

For Val – belated Happy Birthday!

This edition published in 1996 by Lorenz Books
an imprint of Anness Publishing Limited
administration office: 27 West 20th Street
New York, NY 10011

© Anness Publishing Limited

Lorenz Books are available for bulk purchase for sales
promotion and for premium use. For details write or
call the manager of special sales, LORENZ BOOKS,
27 West 20th Street, New York, NY 10011; (212) 807–6739.

Produced by Anness Publishing Limited
1 Boundary Row
London SE1 8HP

ISBN 1 85967 187 X

Publisher: Joanna Lorenz
Project Editor: Judith Simons
Designer: Kit Johnson
Special photography: Lucy Mason
Stylist: Thomasina Smith
Step photography: Shona Wood
Illustrators: Madeleine David and Lucinda Ganderton

Typeset by MC Typeset Limited
Printed and bound in Hong Kong

Contents

Introduction

For many centuries, people of different cultures have hung objects overhead for protection and other purposes: garlic and effigies have been used to ward off evil spirits and the undead; mistletoe has been thought to bring fertility to women. Certain practices continue today, although observance of them often has more to do with tradition than religious belief or superstition. For example, the druidic practice of hanging decorations from oak trees in winter, to encourage tree spirits to return and produce fresh leaves, was replaced in the Christian era with the custom of decorating a fir tree – its triangular shape suggesting the Holy Trinity – which in turn has become a Christmas tradition in the West.

Above:
For druids and Christians hanging objects overhead or from trees has symbolic meaning. From these traditions stem today's glitzy Christmas tree decorations like this gilded mushroom.

Far left:
With its mystical candles flickering away on a damp, wintry day, this naturalistic chandelier conjures up images of ancient ritual gatherings. The pendulums are orange halves, painted gold and covered with moss and starfish.

*Natural materials such
as dried flowers, grasses and
seedheads make charming
mobiles. Easy to make, you simply
insert your chosen material
into a ball of florist's foam.*

Nevertheless, hanging objects, particularly those that move, still have the power to evoke a strong fascination. Pendulums have been used in hypnosis to induce a state of trance. There is still a belief in some quarters that by hanging a pregnant woman's wedding ring from a strand of her hair over her stomach, it is possible to discover the sex of the child she is carrying. If the ring rotates clockwise, the child is a girl; if it rotates counterclockwise, it is a boy. Windchimes are usually these

days decorative, but they originally acted as gentle warning mechanisms. As the wind blows through the chimes they clash together, producing a bell-like tinkling and whistling. If hung outside they warn of approaching bad weather, and if they are hung inside against a door they notify the arrival of visitors as the door is opened. Weathervanes are another wind-assisted weather warning, turning on a pivot with the direction of the wind. Windchimes and weathervanes are clear influences on the modern mobile, both in the way they are presented, hung or on a pivot, and in the way they move, creating different shapes and forms as they do so.

This element of fascination is clearly seen in children's toys. Mexican children still enjoy the ancient custom of the piñatas. These are large papier-mâché objects fashioned as ships, flowers, stars and animals. Covered in tissue paper, they enclose a clay pot filled with fruit and candy. The piñata is

*Weathervanes turn on a pivot
in the same way as some of the
early mobile designs,
pioneered by Alexander Calder.*

suspended from a rope, the children blindfolded and spun round. They then try to beat the piñata with a stick until it cracks and the contents spill to the ground, with the children rushing in to recover the spoils. Other toys linked to mobiles in the way they move or are constructed include puppets which are suspended by thread from a wooden frame; windmill toys; and toys originating in the Far East, which often use wind as a propelling force. It is not surprising that a mobile is often given to a baby as a first toy. When hung over the crib, the movement of the suspended objects, which are often brightly colored, encourages the child to focus on the colors and shapes.

The modern mobile as we know it is a recent phenomenon. Although there are many examples of traditional objects that rely on movement caused by the wind, it was not until the 1930s that mobile sculptures and art forms began to develop in any significant sense. Strongly influenced by the Dutch abstract painter Piet Mondrian's experiments in color, the American painter and designer Alexander Calder began to produce 'mobile' structures consisting of two-dimensional shapes in abstract composition suspended from a wire frame. By surrounding the shapes with light and space Calder introduced a third dimension to his work.

As mobiles gained in popularity, the structures and elements became more complex and, increasingly, three-dimensional shapes were included. Today the range of materials from which mobiles are made is vast. Suspended in the air, delicately balanced to revolve, mobiles simultaneously present many combinations of shape and form.

In a short space of time the mobile has become a form of expression accessible to people of all ages. The mobile is all things to all people: a three-dimensional structure, a plaything, a conversation piece and a constantly changing focal point.

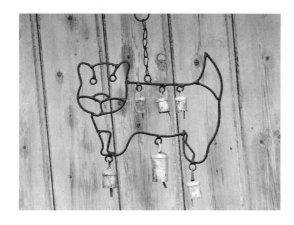

*Windchimes were once
relied upon to forewarn of bad
weather, now we can
simply be soothed by their sound.*

Mobile style

Most mobiles are made of shapes suspended from arms. They usually consist of three elements: the suspended shapes; wire or thread from which the shapes hang; and a framework of wire, bamboo, thin plastic tubing or wood to which the thread or wire is attached.

Not all mobiles are made in this way and some may be hung one component part above another or from a circle, a bar, a cross or a star framework. Sometimes the hanging wires or threads form an integral part of the structure: the wires used to suspend the features of Ofer Acoo's Picasso-inspired face are themselves part of the face. A mobile does not have to be

A wooden crossbar is a popular way to hang a mobile.

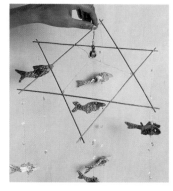

A star-shaped frame provides a rigid symmetrical structure.

Bobbing around at different heights, these sea shapes are suspended from almost invisible threads to increase the sense that they are floating freely in the sea. Most mobiles work best if the shapes are arranged at various levels.

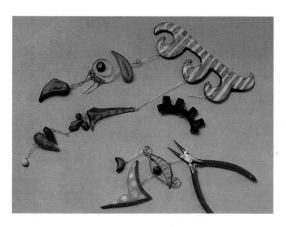

The wiring together of the pieces in this Picasso-inspired mobile is an integral part of the design.

*This borrows an idea from
the first mobile-maker, Alexander
Calder, who balanced his
designs on a pivot point.*

*Above:
Turn a window into something
of a focal point by suspending your
mobile from a drapery pole.
These bold shapes are made from
salt dough, with translucent
hard candies forming the central
"jewels." You could achieve
an equally successful result with
transparent materials such
as glass and plastic.*

suspended. A more unusual construction is based on a pivot, such as that used in Labeena Ishaque's Stabile Face, which in turn is influenced by the work of the first mobile-maker, Alexander Calder, earlier this century.

Where to hang mobiles

A mobile can be hung wherever there is enough space for it to move freely and where it will not look closed in. Mobiles are best hung at eye level. They are often hung from a ceiling, but may also be suspended from the lower part of a lampshade or from a mantelpiece, in a window or in a doorway. Windchimes are ideal for doorways where even the lightest breeze will catch them and make them move. A series of mobiles hung over a cabinet or bookshelf can be used to create a room divider.

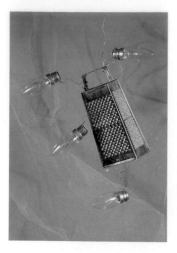

This abstract, surrealist design using a cheese grater and small light bulbs shows how unlikely objects can trigger an idea for a mobile. And, it certainly won't go unnoticed!

Raid your tool box and you could uncover a useful source of mobile parts. This one just goes to prove that a mobile can be "something from nothing."

Above:
As this simple kitchen mobile shows it sometimes pays to let colors give you your lead; here the scarlet chili peppers are the perfect foil for the silver and green.

Opposite:
Take one cake ring . . . Add a handful of dried rose stems and an organdy ribbon, and you have the making of a very pretty mobile. Here the cake ring has been spray-painted gold.

What to hang

Almost anything can be used to create a mobile as long as it is not too heavy. The lighter the object hung, the more easily the mobile will move. Heavy materials such as clay can be used in small amounts or when rolled very thin.

Collect "found" natural objects when out walking, such as dried flowers and fruit, flotsam and jetsam from the beach, feathers, chestnuts and shells. Other "found" objects include toys from crackers, doll's house furniture, miniature dolls and plastic building blocks, even brightly colored children's plastic cups and cutlery. Kitchen utensils can be used to make mobiles, perhaps suspended from skewers and kebab sticks. Try making mobiles by hanging pastry cutters, cookie cutters and other small utensils.

Edible mobile elements from the kitchen might include cinnamon sticks, dried fruit and vegetables such as apples, oranges, chilies and peppers. These look pretty when interspersed with bay leaves and seeds.

Try to look at things with a fresh eye. Don't think, what does this item do? Think, what can I use it for? Knobs, hooks and nails can all be used for hanging objects. The holes in a colander make this kitchen utensil an ideal mobile frame. Butcher's hooks can be linked onto one another. Cup hooks can be screwed into a wooden crosspiece to make a mobile for the kitchen. Even a cheese grater has holes in it which could be put to good use.

Festive mobiles

Mobiles are an inexpensive way of decorating for festive occasions. For example, if you want to fill a room with flowers and it is the wrong season, make flowers from paper, felt or papier-mâché and hang them as mobiles to make a colorful display. At Christmas suspend balls from crossed coat-hangers wrapped in tinsel and hang them all around the house. At Easter hang painted blown eggs from the branch of a tree with ribbons.

Construction techniques

Shapes for hanging

Mobiles can be made from almost any light material which can be suspended. Florist's foam is light and easy to carve. Cotton balls can be painted and decorated with beads and sequins to make glittering ornaments. Papier-mâché shapes are easily made from the most readily available of materials – old newspaper. Papier-mâché can be used in combination with other materials to fill out the form. For example, it is applied to carved florist's foam pieces in the Under the Sea project to make fish, and to cardboard in the Palmistry project. Perhaps the easiest mobiles are those made from shapes cut from card. Sewn fabric and felt animal and toy shapes make brightly colored mobiles for babies and children.

You'll need flour, salt and wallpaper paste to make salt dough, which handles well for being molded or cut into shapes, such as these leaves. Cookie dough is an edible alternative.

Florist's foam is easy to carve into three-dimensional shapes. Use a craft knife or whatever helps you achieve the shape you want. Before you start, pause to think about the overall scale, and even make a few shallow cuts to remind you where one section stops, so you don't run out of foam.

Felt is an excellent choice for a mobile which is going to hang in a child's room or nursery. Available in bright colors, it is easy to cut and soft to touch. Don't feel that felt is an option only for youngsters though; if you stick to bright red and green you have the beginning of a mobile for Christmas.

Papier-mâché is really useful for filling out a shape from your initial flat outline, such as the hand being worked here. Wads of newspaper, taped in place, provide the form, which is then smoothly covered with strips of newspaper applied, layer by layer, with wallpaper paste.

Above:
Children love to watch
glittery and shiny materials
sway and catch the light.

Right:
The "edible kitchen" provides
lots of inspiration for mobiles.
Dried slices of fruit and
herbs can all be put to use.

Collect candy wrappers, bits of broken china, ribbons and beads for decorating mobile pieces. When a mobile is to be hung near a window, make full use of the light source by choosing reflective materials. Sequins, colored cellophane, plexiglas, glass beads and gems, tiny mirrors and glittery beads will all catch the light and draw attention towards the mobile.

More unusual materials for mobile pieces include baked salt dough and cookies (for more temporary mobiles). Modeling clay can be used in small amounts. Dried fruits and flowers, herbs and spices make pretty mobile elements for the kitchen.

Mobile frames

The most traditional frame for a mobile is made up of a series of bars suspended from a long central bar. Materials to use include dowelling, knitting needles, skewers, kebab sticks, bamboo canes, pencils and chopsticks.

Crossbars are a popular way of hanging mobiles with five hanging shapes. Hang a shape from the end of each arm and the fifth from the center. Crossbars can be made from wood, cardboard or wire. Wooden crossbars are made more solid if a rabbet or groove is cut in the center of each bar before gluing together. Add a tack, or bind with thread to form a strong joint.

A circular frame can be made from wire, card or the stiffener used for boning theatrical costumes. The circle can then be painted or covered in fabric. For a small mobile, a large curtain ring might be suitable.

Try choosing a frame which fits the theme of the mobile. The planets of the Lost in Space project are hung from a globe paper lampshade. The dolls in the Peg Doll Family are hung from a piece of broom handle cut into a peg shape. A papier-mâché colander forms the frame for the Colander and Vegetables project. The shapes in the Iced Cookies project are tied to holes drilled in a wooden spoon.

For a crossbar frame, first glue your two bars together.

To secure firmly, bind the joint tightly with thread.

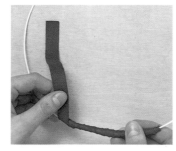

Conceal a circular wire frame with paint or cover it in fabric.

Keep the theme of your mobile in mind when planning its frame and you should find you can enhance the frame itself with some clever techniques! Here, this jovial magician looks as if he and his friends are enjoying center stage beneath a brightly colored canopy.

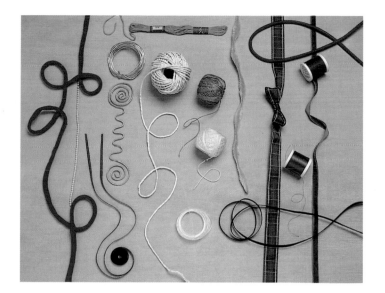

Be creative with your choice of threads for your mobile.

This mobile comes together as a whole largely because the silver chains work so well with the fish molds. The overall effect is that of an old-fashioned pair of kitchen scales.

If you intend to hang your shapes from a length of fairly rigid wire, you can always attach a separate, more malleable, wire loop to hook your frame on to.

A double knot fastens the shape so that it is ready to be attached to the frame. Fishing line is an excellent choice as it is both strong and, being transparent, virtually invisible.

Threads and wires

Although often an afterthought, the thread or wire chosen to hang the shapes is an important element of the overall design of a mobile. If you wish the parts of the mobile to appear to float freely in the air, use an invisible thread such as nylon fishing line, which has the additional benefit of being very strong. Brightly colored shapes can be hung from contrasting embroidery silk, wool or cord. Elastic is ideal for a mobile that is to be hung across a baby carriage or play pen. As well as traditional corded and sewing elastic, more decorative elastics are available which include colored threads, lace or glitter in

their construction. Chains and ribbons might be chosen to fit in with the theme of a mobile.

Wire is the best choice for a more structured, controlled mobile. Wires used in the projects include galvanized wire, florist's wire, jewelry wire and coat-hangers. The ends of the hanging wires can be bent into hooks to fit into holes made in the frame and pieces.

The hanging threads can be decorated with beads and sequins. Tie knots in the thread to space the beads as required. More than one mobile piece can be hung on the same thread. Pass the crinkled part of a flexible drinking straw down the thread for the piece to rest on.

Hooks for hanging

Mobiles can be hung from small screw hooks or larger cup hooks. Light mobiles can be hung from a wire loop attached to a hollow wall anchor. Heavier mobiles are best hung from a wooden frame like a doorway or shelf. Use screw inserts when screwing hooks into the wall or ceiling to keep them from falling out.

The balancing act!
Make sure your mobile is in its
final position, as drafts
and even room temperature
can affect how it hangs.

Inspired no doubt by the
psychic powers of Yuri Geller, this
mobile relies on all kinds
of hooks, wiring and pieces of
twisted metal to link it together.

Tools and equipment

The projects in the book require a wide range of basic craft techniques, including sewing, papier-mâché, beadwork, crochet and baking. Most of the tools and equipment are readily available in the home; pens, pencils, ruler, craft knife or scalpel, scissors, paintbrushes, needles, pliers and wire cutters are the tools most often used. A piece of thick cardboard serves very well as a cutting mat, and plates and bowls can be used for mixing paints and wallpaper paste. More specific tools are needed for some projects. A soldering iron and glass cutter are used to make the glass panels in the Partridge in a Pear Tree project. The loops in the wire for the Picasso-influenced face are made using jeweler's pliers.

Balancing mobiles

Balancing the finished mobile can be the most frustrating part of any project. Often, trial and error is the only way to achieve a perfect balance, but you can bear the following points in mind. Shapes hung from a crossbar or ring need to be evenly spaced if they are of equal weight. Shapes of different weight can be moved along the bars or around the ring until the mobile hangs evenly. Use a sliding knot in the thread while you are adjusting the mobile and then tie it securely once you are happy with the overall balance.

*You can even go as far
as to paint the background wall
with a scene suited to
your mobile.*

Heavenly bodies

mobiles with a celestial theme

As mobiles are usually suspended above our heads and to view them we must shift our gaze skywards, it seems particularly appropriate to have a chapter on astral mobiles. Whether your particular interest is in astronomy or astrology, there will be something here to your liking – the weather with its thunder and lightning, palmistry and astrological symbols, a mystical temple, and starry planets with a burning sun.

Artists' gallery

S u n   f a c e

*The ever-popular sun
motif has been given an
unusual dimension by attaching
small cow-bells to its points.
(People and Planet)*

S u n s   a n d   m o o n s

*Metallic suns, moons and bells
hang close enough together to make
this mobile a tinkling windchime.
(People and Planet)*

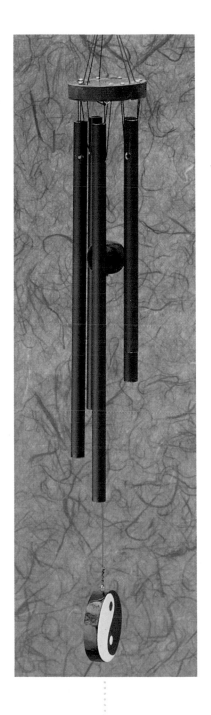

Yin and Yang

*The two interdependent but
opposing principles of Chinese
philosophy are represented in
the Yin and Yang symbol. Here it
is suspended beneath
an elegant windchime.
(People and Planet)*

Celestial

*This heavenly mobile featuring
a cherub, the sun, the moon and
stars is made from white plastic.
(Louise Slater)*

Instant inspiration

Solar system

*Create a miniature planetarium
by suspending balls from a dome-
shaped wire frame. Spray-paint
some of the balls silver.*

Spaceships

*Spray-paint shuttlecocks
silver and hang them from a length
of glittery plastic tubing to
create the appearance of rockets
shooting into space.*

Star bright

The metallic colors and geometric shapes of many kitchen utensils make them interesting mobile pieces. Hang pastry cutters from a tin can for a glittering space-age mobile.

Capricorn

Stick animal-shaped kitchen molds and gold stars around a ring of cardboard. Suspend the animal or symbol representing your star sign from the ring to make your own personal zodiac.

Lost in space

The earth and the planets beyond are encompassed in this mobile. Balloons form the basis of the fiery sun and brilliant planets.

tools and materials

balloons | newspaper | wallpaper paste | thin cardboard | scissors | masking tape | acrylic paints | paintbrushes | glitter glue | galvanized wire | globe paper lampshade | snub-nosed pliers | fishing line | needle |

1 Blow up four small balloons to the size of your palm. Apply several layers of newspaper strips with wallpaper paste. Allow the paper to dry.

2 Cut out a strip of thin cardboard, about 4 in wide and long enough to go around the circumference of one of the balloons. Cut a row of curved rays along one long edge of the cardboard and a row of tabs along the other. Wrap the cardboard strip around the balloon, taping down the tabs. You may find it easier to attach the cardboard if you cut it in half first. Then cover the cardboard with more strips of newspaper and wallpaper paste.

3 Paint this balloon in red and yellow to look like the sun. Paint the other balloons in bright, bold colors and decorate with glitter glue. Wrap a long length of galvanized wire around one of the planets to form planet rings.

4 Thread two pieces of wire approximately 20 in long through the globe lampshade to form a cross.

5 Using snub-nosed pliers, form a hook at each end of the wires. Attach the planets and stars to the lampshade using fishing line.

The globe-shaped paper lampshade printed with the map of the world makes the perfect frame from which to hang papier-mâché planets. (Labeena Ishaque)

Simply stars

Stars are a very striking
and popular motif. Here hung from
a simple ring, sequins and
glitter glue add sparkle.

tools and materials

cardboard | craft knife | gold and silver spray paint |
glitter glue | star-shaped sequins | silver beads |
needle | glitter thread | red and gold ribbon |
wooden ring, 4 in in diameter | white glue |

*The pretty cascade of glittering
stars is easy to make from
cardboard sprayed with gold and
silver paint. (Janet Bridge)*

1 Cut out several star
shapes from cardboard,
in two different sizes. Spray
paint the stars gold on one
side and silver on the other.

2 Decorate one side of
the stars with glitter
glue and allow to dry. Then
turn over and decorate the
other side.

3 Thread star-shaped
sequins and silver
beads onto the glitter thread,
knotting as you go to space
the beads along the thread.
Add the stars by pushing the
needle through the cardboard
and knotting the thread. Make
a decorated length of about
21 in, then make another two
lengths that are slightly
shorter.

4 Wrap red and gold
ribbon around the
wooden ring, attaching it with
glue. Tie the stars to the ring
and then tie three lengths of
glitter thread to the top and
knot together for hanging.

Weather

Bright sunshine and stormy rain clouds balance either side of this mobile, bridged by a colorful rainbow.

tools and materials

pencil | *felt scraps in a variety of colors* | *scissors* | *cotton batting* | *fabric glue* | *paintbrush* | *needle* | *embroidery thread* | *thin cardboard* | *double-sided sticky tape* |

1 Draw the outlines of the simple weather shapes – a cloud, sun, moon, rainbow, raindrops and a lightning bolt – on the felt. Cut out two of each shape.

2 Sandwich batting between each pair of shapes and glue down the edges. Sew a running stitch around the edges using embroidery thread.

3 Attach a length of thread to the top of the sun, and one joining the sun and moon. Sew raindrops onto the cloud, leaving thread between the drops and the cloud. Attach the lightning bolt to the cloud in the same way. Sew thread to the top of the rainbow and cloud for hanging.

4 Roll the cardboard to make a thin rod. Cover the rod with felt, holding it in place with double-sided sticky tape. Tie the weather motifs to the rod so that they hang at different levels.

You'll find a weather symbol to match your mood on this hand-stitched felt mobile, whatever the weather outside.
(Labeena Ishaque)

Palmistry

Stars, spirals and rings
spring from this mystical hand.
The vibrant decoration is enhanced
with light-reflecting mirror glass.

tools and materials

cardboard | craft knife | newspaper | masking tape |
galvanized wire | wire cutters | snub-nosed pliers |
wallpaper paste | mirror glass | hammer | plastic body
filler | white glue | white acrylic primer |
paintbrushes | liquid gold leaf paint | gloss polyurethane
varnish | small brass screw hooks | epoxy resin glue |
acrylic paints | small brass jump rings | picture wire |

1 Use the templates from the back of the book to cut out the winged hand and all the component shapes from cardboard. Crumple small pieces of newspaper and tape them to each shape to create the form. Leave the wings of the hand and the small stars flat. Using the snub-nosed pliers, coil and bend a piece of wire, following the template at the back of the book, and tape to the sun shape.

2 Using wallpaper paste, cover each shape in several layers of newspaper. Allow to dry.

3 Break the mirror by placing it between several sheets of newspaper and hitting it gently with a hammer. Mix the plastic body filler according to the manufacturer's instructions. Apply to one side of each wing and along the top of the hand, then carefully press in the pieces of mirror. Allow to dry and repeat on the other side of the wings. Stick one small piece of mirror onto each of the small star shapes if desired.

4 Cut five lengths of wire and coil into elaborate "S" shapes following the templates at the back of the book. Coat them with white glue, acrylic primer, gold paint and finally varnish, leaving to dry between each stage. Screw one small hook into each of the papier-mâché shapes, into the tip of each finger and into each wing of the hand. Screw four into the sun piece. Secure the hooks with epoxy resin glue. Coat the shapes with white glue, then with acrylic primer.

5 Paint each shape using acrylic paints and then decorate with gold paint. Let dry.

6 Varnish with gloss polyurethane varnish and allow to dry. Suspend the smaller shapes from the hand using the jump rings to attach them. Suspend the larger shapes from three of the wire coils and hang these from the hand. Attach the remaining wire coils to the wings. Attach the small stars to the sun piece. Thread a length of picture wire through the two coils on the wings for hanging.

The ancient art of palm-reading is symbolized in this exquisite papier-mâché and wire construction. (Kim Rowley)

Bead temple

Curved and coiled wire forms a pretty and deceptively strong structure for the shimmering iridescent beadwork.

tools and materials

4 yd fine gold-plated wire | *wire cutters* | *snub-nosed pliers* | *3 yd glass rocaille beads* | *beading needle* | *strong bonded nylon thread* | *scissors* | *large bead* | *swivel* |

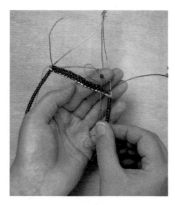

1 Cut a length of wire, twist it into a double circle and flatten it out into a triangle. Cut three pieces of wire, bend an open loop on one end of each length and close onto the corners of the triangle frame with snub-nosed pliers. Tie the free ends together at the top.

Cut three pieces of wire and bend into "V" shapes. Thread with beads up to where the wire will pivot on the triangle frame. Attach one "V" to one side of the pyramid base by twisting the free wire over and under the triangle frame, as shown here.

2 To make the beaded pyramid sides, thread a beading needle with a long length of strong thread. To attach the beads, use the following technique, known as brick stitch. Tie the thread around a bead, making two knots. Pass the thread under one side of the triangle frame and back up through the bead. Pick up another bead and attach it to the wire in the same way. Continue in this manner until you are one bead's width away from the other corner. To strengthen the base row, go back through every bead, passing the thread under the wire as you go.

3 Pick up the first bead of the second row and let it fall to the end of the thread. Pass the needle through the loop joining the first and second beads of the base row. Take the thread back into your working bead, on the same side that the thread came out. Pick up another bead and join it on in the same way. Continue until the second row is one bead shorter than the base row.

Pick up a bead – this will be an "edge" bead – and let it fall to the end of the thread. Take the needle down through the end bead of the base row, around the wire and back up through the end bead of the base row and the edge bead, as shown.

4 Take the thread up and down through each bead in the row in turn until you reach the other end. Then attach an edge bead on that end in the same way. This allows a small gap so that there is space for the wires to pivot. Continue threading beads in brick stitch until your triangle is complete. Remember that each row should be one row shorter than the preceding row. Attach a "V" to the second side of the triangle and bead the next side of the pyramid as before, and then complete the third side in the same way.

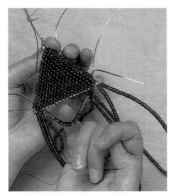

5 Take a short length of doubled thread and tie a large bead onto a swivel – make it very secure as the whole mobile will be hanging from this swivel. Tie a new thread onto one of the edge beads and sew the beaded triangles together up the edges and over the wires to complete the pyramid. Enclose the large bead and the base of the swivel when you sew the last side up.

Make a short and a long swinger from thread and beads to suspend from each side of the triangle frame. Tie and knot them securely to the frame.

6 Using pliers, bend the projecting wires into spirals at the top of the pyramid. Fix beads to each curled end. Tie strong thread onto the swivel for hanging.

The architecture of Ancient Greece is brought to mind by this marvelous beadwork and sculpted wire mobile. (Debbie Siniska)

Celestial celebrations

mobiles for special occasions

Everyone everywhere celebrates important dates at some time or another, be it a birth, marriage, birthday or traditional seasonal festivities, or perhaps moving house or passing a driving test. A celebration calls for flamboyant decorations, so mark the occasion with a suitable mobile.

Artists' gallery

Little houses

This Columbian spiraling windchime is made of clay. Each part is a little house, making the mobile a charming housewarming gift. (People and Planet)

Indian wedding

The elephant is a symbol used at Hindu weddings. This string of elephants was made in India and is brightly decorated for a celebration. (People and Planet)

Cat bells

*An animal-shaped mobile
makes an unusual gift for someone
celebrating the arrival or
birthday of a pet. This metal cat is
decorated with cow-bells.
(People and Planet)*

Angelic hosts

*A naïve art mobile of
papier-mâché angels and stars.
(Jan Barber/Papier Marché)*

Instant inspiration

Fairy lights

*Christmas decorations such
as tree lights and ornaments are
an obvious and effective choice
for a homemade seasonal mobile.*

Partytime

*Trumpets and streamers
make a lively birthday mobile.*

Easter basket

*Fill a plastic bucket with
tissue paper and add a cluster of
Easter eggs. Suspend more
eggs from around the edges of
the basket.*

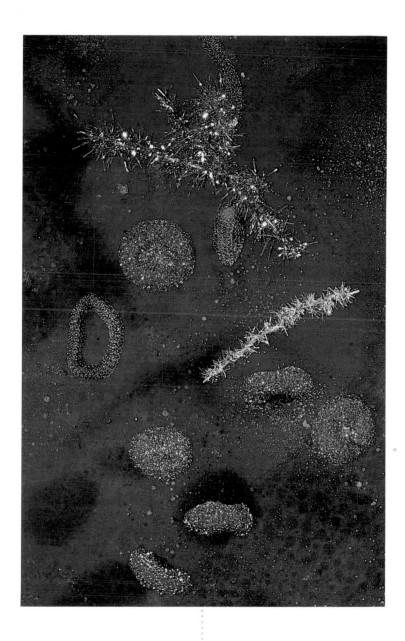

N o e l

*Hang wire kitchen scrubbers
from tinsel-covered bars to make
an alternative decoration that
still has lots of Christmas sparkle.*

Christmas wreaths

Celebrate a family Christmas with a mobile made from simple pantry ingredients and traditional seasonal imagery.

tools and materials

1 cup flour | 1 cup salt | 1 tbsp oil | 1 tbsp wallpaper paste powder | large mixing bowl | rolling pin | holly leaf pastry cutter | foil | baking sheet | acrylic paints | paintbrushes | clear varnish | strong glue or glue gun | 1/4 in wide red ribbon | 1/8 in wide green ribbon | brass ring |

1 Make a salt dough using the flour, salt, oil and wallpaper paste. Knead the dough thoroughly, divide into two portions and set one aside. Take a third of the dough and divide into three equal portions. Divide each of these in two and roll into two thin sausage shapes. Twist together and join to form three small wreaths. Using the half portion of dough set aside, roll two long, thin sausage shapes and twist to form a large wreath. Make eight evenly spaced holes around the large wreath and a small hole in each of the small wreaths.

2 Take half of the remaining dough and make three icicles by folding rolled lengths of dough in half and twisting. Leave a gap where you start twisting for threading the ribbon.

3 Roll out the remaining dough and cut out four holly leaves using the pastry cutter. Roll some tiny berries from the trimmings. Make a small hole in each leaf and shape over foil. Allow all the pieces to dry. Place the shapes on a baking sheet and bake in an oven at 250°F for 6 to 8 hours.

4 Paint the icicles, the holly leaves and the berries with acrylic paint. Allow the paint to dry and then varnish.

5 Glue the holly leaves in pairs and add the berries to them.

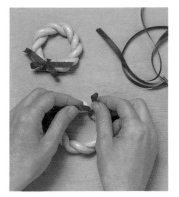

6 Tie a red ribbon bow to each small wreath.

7 Cut the green ribbon into 12 in lengths and tie a knot 5½ in along each length. Thread the ribbons through the holes in the large wreath and tie one end of each to the brass ring for hanging. Tie the leaves, icicles and wreaths to the other ends of the ribbons.

The traditional Christmas wreath is injected with new life when combined with icicles and holly leaves to make a mobile. Seasonally colored red and green ribbons have been chosen for hanging and decorating the salt dough shapes. (Dorothy Wood)

Folk art angels

Inspired by Pennsylvania-Dutch imagery, these angels are simple to make and a pretty way to herald Christmas.

tools and materials

cardboard | double-sided sticky tape | floral print cotton scraps | black and gold felt scraps | fine and thick black marker pens | fine cord | hacksaw | wooden knitting needle | 2 brass backing circles | 2 brass knobs | strong glue or glue gun |

The jaunty shapes of the angels make an uplifting Christmas mobile reminiscent of folk art. (Lucinda Ganderton)

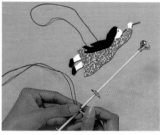

4 Attach a length of cord to each angel. Using a hacksaw, cut off the knob and the point from either end of the knitting needle and slide on the two brass backing circles. Then glue a brass knob onto each end of the needle. Tie a length of cord around the center of the needle and glue the backing circles together to cover the knot. Finally, tie two angels to each side of the needle.

1 Make four angels in the same way. Using the template at the back of the book, cut out the angel figure from cardboard. Using the same template cut two templates from cardboard, one for the dress and one for the hair.

2 Stick double-sided sticky tape onto the back of the printed cotton fabric and draw around the dress template. Reverse the template to draw around the second dress piece. Cut out and glue a dress piece onto each side of the angel's body.

3 Cut hair from black felt and stick a piece to each side of the head. Cut out and stick on shoes and a gold trumpet. Draw the eyes with the fine marker. Color the cardboard edges showing between the pieces of black felt with the thick marker.

Christmas cans

Punched tin is a traditional Mexican craft. Choose simple shapes that are easy to cut.

tools and materials

wax crayon | 2 empty, smooth sided tin cans | paper | sticky tape | can opener | wooden block | punch | hammer | tin snips | metal polish | string |

1 With the wax crayon, draw the design of holes to be punched, using the tin can template at the back of the book as a guide. Attach the paper to one can with sticky tape. Remove the can's lid and base and insert the wooden block. Punch holes using the punch and hammer. Keep moving the block so that you are always banging the punch into it.

2 Remove the lid and base from the second can and cut through it using tin snips.

4 Tape the shapes onto a wooden block and punch the pattern of holes onto the surface. Polish the shapes and the can with metal polish. Use lengths of string to suspend the shapes from the can and to hang the mobile.

3 Using the tin shape templates, draw the shapes and the punched design on paper and tape to the opened can. Use tin snips to cut out the shapes.

An alternative Christmas decoration for those tired of tinsel and ornaments, this mobile is made from two tin cans.
(Dorothy Wood)

Birthday cake

Sugar-almond colors and tissue-paper flowers have been chosen to decorate this cake mobile.

tools and materials

colored cardboard | *scissors* | *white glue* | *poster paints* | *sponge* | *paintbrush* | *colored tissue papers* | *narrow ribbon* | *colored threads* |

1 Make three cake tiers in different sizes. For each tier, cut out two circles from cardboard, both the same size, and a cardboard strip as long as the circumference of the circles. Remember to leave tabs on the circles.

2 Curve the cardboard strip around one of the circles and glue the tabs to the inside of the strip. Glue the second circle to the other edge of the strip.

3 Decorate the tiers using poster paints. Apply color to the top of each tier with a sponge and add a trellis pattern around the sides with a paintbrush.

4 Cut the tissue paper into small squares, crumple them into balls and glue around the top edge of each tier.

5 Using the narrow ribbon, tie little bows and glue onto the cake tiers.

6 Cut candle shapes from cardboard and paint on the yellow flames. Cut the bottom ends into points. Make slits in the top of the smallest cake tier and insert the candles.

7 Find the center of each tier and pierce a small hole. Suspend the tiers one above the other using short threads. Attach a thread to the center of the top tier for hanging.

However old the birthday girl or boy, they'll love this colorful cake mobile. For a child's birthday, make a tier for every year of their life. (Melanie Williams)

Chinese banners

Miniature silk banners in rich colors have been decorated with oriental calligraphy and hung from bamboo sticks.

tools and materials

silk fabric scraps | scissors | gold thread | needle | sewing machine | iron | 8 bamboo skewers, 2 × 8 in and 6 × 4¾ in long | gold metallic pen |

What better way to herald the New Year or the arrival of spring than with the crisp, uncluttered forms of Chinese banners?
(Labeena Ishaque)

1 Cut out four pieces of silk, one 12 × 7 in and the other three pieces 8 × 4 in. Using the gold thread, blanket stitch along the longer sides of each rectangle. Turn the right sides together and machine stitch the shorter ends together.

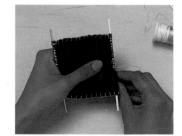

2 Turn the right way out and press with a cool iron. Insert two bamboo skewers inside each fabric pocket. Using gold thread, sew around the skewers tightly, so that one is at the top and one at the bottom.

3 Using a gold metallic pen, draw some Chinese characters on the silk. Leave to dry and then decorate the other side.

4 Assemble the mobile using the gold thread and a needle. Hang the three smaller banners from the large one, so that the central small banner is lower than the other two.

Captured harvest

A mobile of dried flowers
and grasses makes an apt decoration
for a harvest festival or
Thanksgiving dinner.

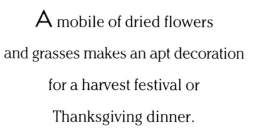

tools and materials

medium gauge florist's wire | wire cutters | 3 florist's foam balls | dried moss | raffia | selection of dried flowers and grasses | scissors | tweezers |

1 Cut several short lengths of medium-gauge florist's wire and bend them to make small staples. Cover the florist's foam balls with dried moss, securing it with the staples. Make sure that the staples and foam balls are completely camouflaged.

2 Bend a piece of florist's wire into a hook and use it to pull a length of raffia through the center of each ball. Knot the raffia at the bottom to stop it pulling all the way through.

3 Snip some dried flowers and grasses into small pieces. Using a pair of tweezers, push the stalks into the florist's foam until all the balls are covered. Complete one area at a time.

4 Space the balls evenly along the raffia and tie on small pieces of raffia to keep them in position. Finish off the mobile with a raffia bow at the top.

*Nature's bounty is celebrated
in the arrangement of dried moss,
grasses and flowers.
(Janet Bridge)*

Entirely
individual

mobiles reflecting favorite hobbies

Creating a mobile to represent someone's abiding passion for, say birdwatching, arts and crafts, travel or archeology, is a wonderful and individual idea for a gift. The mobile can be suspended in their workroom or bedroom as a constant reminder of their special interest. If your hobby is crafts, you will find mobiles made using a wide variety of techniques, including papier-mâché, basic carpentry, clay modeling and decoupage.

Artists' gallery

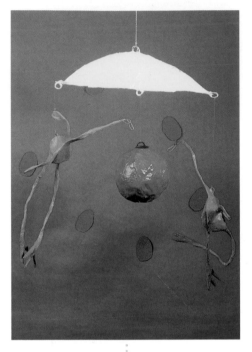

Flamingoes

*Eccentric pink birds fly around
a globe under a bright yellow
canopy. A mobile for ornithologists
with an eye for the unusual.*
(James Dean)

Ballet steps

*This rather plump dancer
surrounded by her exotic animals
makes a fun mobile for
dancers with a sense of humor.*
(Jim Edminston/Lucky Parrot)

Honey-bee

*This giant hanging bee would
strike fear into the hearts of all but
the most dedicated of beekeepers.
(Bridget Hinge/Papier Marché)*

Music

*A noteworthy mobile that
will delight musicians, the musical
symbols are suspended
from a wire stave.
(Louise Slater)*

Instant inspiration

Card sharks

*Suspend playing cards
randomly from wooden bars so
that they appear to be falling
through the air.*

Clockworks

*A mobile for horologists,
delicate watch and clock parts are
suspended from twisted wire.*

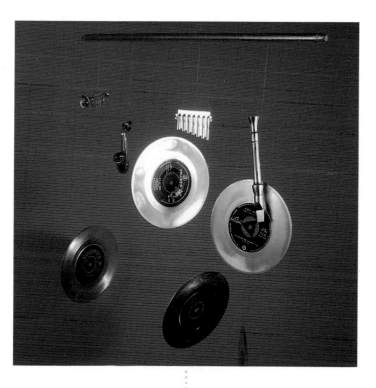

Green fingers

*For the gardener, cover a
coat-hanger in artificial turf and
flowers. Hang miniature tools
from this flowery lawn.*

Music buffs

*Record collectors will love
this musical mobile. Hang records
and miniature instruments at
different levels from a single bar.*

Arts and crafts

With its useful equipment strung from an artist's palette, this would make a great gift for a craft aficionado. Vary the hanging elements to reflect their particular interests.

tools and materials

craft knife | *thick cardboard* | *acrylic paints* | *paintbrush* | *fine-grade sandpaper* | *thin cardboard* | *scissors* | *twine* | *white glue* | *small ball* | *petroleum jelly* | *newspaper* | *wallpaper paste* | *white latex paint* | *thick paper* | *fine black marker pen* | *silver spray paint* | *brass paper fastener* | *dressmaker's pins* | *thread* |

1 Use a craft knife to cut out a palette shape from thick cardboard. Using acrylic paints, paint it a woody color and allow to dry. Spatter it with another color or sand it lightly. Add blotches of paint around the palette.

2 Draw and cut out two simple paintbrush shapes from thin cardboard. Cut some short lengths of twine, fray them and glue them along the edge of one of the brush shapes. For the pincushion, coat the ball in petroleum jelly. Cover the ball with several layers of newspaper strips and wallpaper paste. Sandwich the two brush shapes together and secure with glue. Cover the brush with layers of newspaper strips and wallpaper paste and allow the pieces to dry.

3 Once fully dry, snip open the papier-mâché pincushion and remove the ball. Smooth the cut edges with sandpaper and stick them back together. Paint with white latex. Once this is dry, decorate with acrylic paints to look like a patchwork pincushion.

4 Draw and cut out the scissor shapes in two pieces from thin cardboard. Cut out a rectangle and two circles for the cotton reel. Roll the rectangle into a cylindrical shape and secure. Then stick a circle to each end to make the cotton reel. Cut a long, thin strip of paper to make a tape measure and then draw the measurements along both sides with a fine black marker pen.

5 Coil up the tape measure. Spray the two scissor shapes silver and secure together with a brass paper fastener. Stick pins into the papier-mâché pincushion and wind thread around the cotton reel.

6 Attach threads to the cotton reel, tape measure, scissors, paintbrush and pincushion. Make small holes around the palette and tie the hanging elements to it.

The ingenious idea of hanging the artist's tools from a palette helps to harmonize the disparate elements of this cardboard and papier-mâché mobile. (Melanie Williams)

Bird watching

This charming and colorful
mobile features elegant
papier-mâché birds in full flight
– a perfect gift for an
ornithologist and an eye-catching
decoration in its own right.

tools and materials

*thick cardboard | craft knife | newspaper | masking
tape | wallpaper paste | paintbrushes | 2 cut-out eye
images | white glue | mirror glass | hammer | plastic
body filler | white acrylic primer | galvanized wire |
wire cutters | snub-nosed pliers | small brass screw hooks |
epoxy resin glue | acrylic paints | gloss polyurethane
varnish | liquid gold leaf paint | small brass jump rings |
gold picture hanging wire |*

1 Using the templates at
the back of the book, cut
out the bird shapes, the
central motif and the heart
perch from thick cardboard.
Crumple and roll small
pieces of newspaper and tape
them to the bird and perch
shapes to create the form.
Tape tiny balls of newspaper
along the top edges of the
central motif. Apply layers of
newspaper with wallpaper
paste to give the shapes a
smooth finish. Allow to dry.
Glue an eye image, taken
from a magazine, on either
side of the central motif.

2 Place the mirror
between several sheets
of newspaper and hit it gently
with a hammer. Apply an
even coating of plastic body
filler to one side of the central
motif. Carefully press in the
small pieces of broken
mirror. Allow to dry and
repeat on the other side. Coat
all the pieces with white glue
and acrylic primer, but don't
cover the mirror pieces.
Using pliers, bend six lengths
of galvanized wire into
elaborate "S" shapes using
the templates at the back of
the book. Screw the small
hooks into the papier-mâché
shapes and secure them with
epoxy resin glue.

3 Paint the designs with
acrylic paints. Once
they are dry, apply two coats
of gloss polyurethane
varnish. Coat the "S" shapes
with white glue, acrylic
primer, gold leaf paint and
finally varnish.

4 When dry, assemble
the mobile by attaching
the jump rings to the small
brass hooks and threading
through the wire "S" shapes.
Attach the gold picture wire
to the two wire pieces at the
top of the mobile, for
hanging.

*Make an indoor aviary
with a flock of brilliantly painted
papier-mâché birds.
(Kim Rowley)*

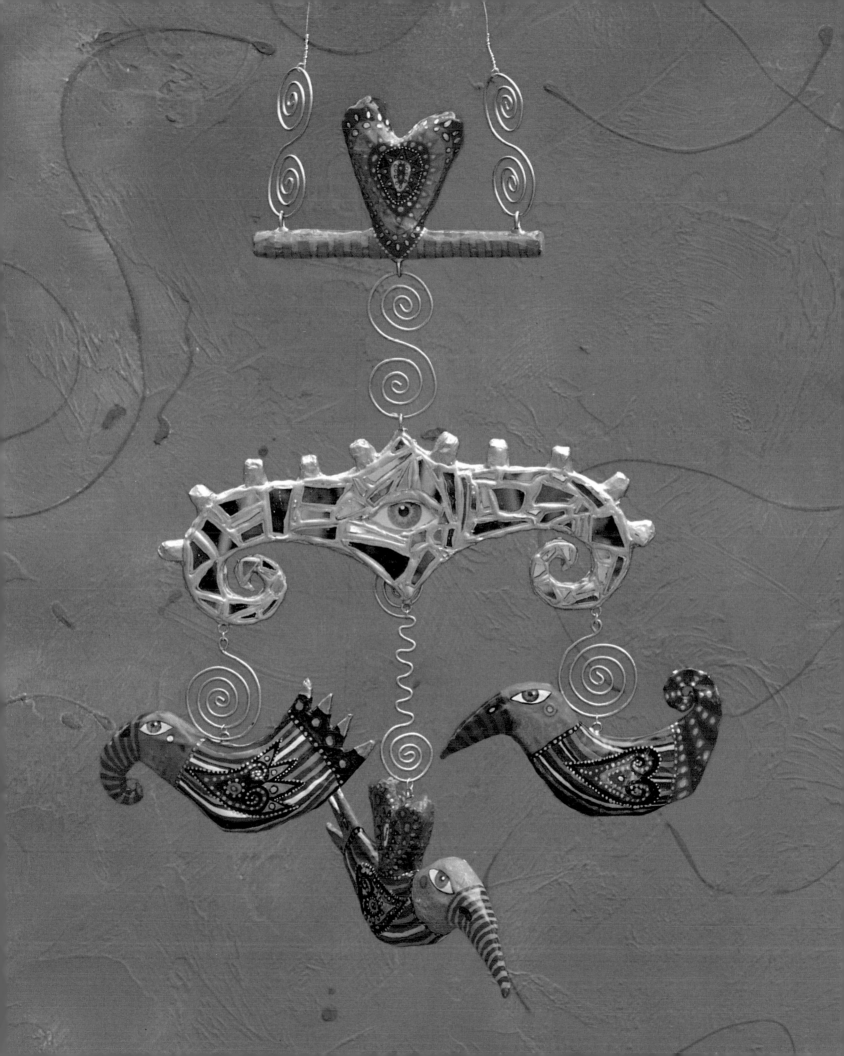

Up in the clouds

The perfect gift for plane spotters of all ages. Vary the theme to create a car or train mobile.

tools and materials

airplane images | *scissors* | *pencil* | *thin white cardboard* | *glue* | *needle* | *cotton knitting yarn* |

Evoke the excitement of air travel with this easy-to-make decoupage mobile. (Josephine Whitfield)

1 Cut out several large and small plane images. Draw and cut out two large clouds and three small clouds from thin cardboard.

2 Glue the small planes onto both sides of the small clouds.

3 With a needle, pierce a hole at the top of each small cloud. Thread lengths of cotton yarn through the holes, knotting them securely.

4 Evenly space out the small clouds then spread glue over one side of the large clouds. Lay the threads from the small clouds onto one glued side, then glue down the other large cloud to sandwich the threads between the two. Pierce a hole at the top of the cloud and attach a length of yarn for hanging. Glue large planes on each side of the large cloud, to finish.

Mobile phones

The ultimate status symbol
for those who love their "mobiles"
and enjoy a play on words.

tools and materials

small piece of ³/₁₆ in plywood | coping saw | fine-grade sandpaper | craft knife | hammer | nail | pliers | acrylic paints | paintbrush | white glue | thread | small brass ring |

1 Use the templates at the back of the book to draw five telephones, dials and crossbars on the plywood. Using a coping saw, cut out the shapes. Sand off the rough edges with sandpaper.

2 Using a craft knife, make shallow notches in the crossbars at both ends. Hammer a nail through the top of each telephone to make a hole. Pull out the nail with a pair of pliers.

3 Paint the telephones and crossbars with acrylic paint. Paint the dials white. Glue the dials onto the phones with white glue.

4 Tie a thread to each telephone and secure with glue. Attach the telephones to the crossbars. Tie thread loosely to the center of each crossbar and move along the bar until it is balanced. Tie, and secure with glue. Attach the mobile to the top crossbar. Tie a thread to the center of the top crossbar and balance.

The current preoccupation with communications is cleverly parodied by these very traditional-looking "mobile" phones. (Al Brown)

Egyptology

Ancient Egyptian symbols and figurative art inspired this beautiful mobile. The central falcon is richly decorated with tiny slices of rolled polymer clay.

tools and materials

polymer clay | *rolling pin* | *craft knife* | *needle* | *galvanized wire* | *snub-nosed pliers* | *burnt umber acrylic paint* | *cloth* | *sandpaper* | *hook* | *gold thread* | *selection of small glass beads* | *mobile crosspiece* |

1 Knead the polymer clay before use. Make several two-color canes. Roll thin rods between your hands. Then roll thin sheets of polymer clay of a different color with a rolling pin and wrap around the rods. Roll evenly to reduce the diameter. To make the beads for hanging, cut some of the canes into thick slices, pierce a hole in each with a needle and bake according to the manufacturer's instructions. Put to one side with the spare canes.

2 Roll out thin sheets of champagne-colored and transparent clay. Layer them, compress, cut and mold into tablet shapes, with rounded corners. Smooth the edges of the tablet pieces and, using wire, make a small hole in the top and three small holes in the base of each.

Bend short lengths of wire into "Egyptian symbols" with snub-nosed pliers. Impress these symbols into the surface of the tablets. Bake the tablets.

3 Smooth burnt umber acrylic paint over the tablets, making sure it gets into all the crevices. Wipe the surface with a damp cloth to remove most of the paint and to create an "antique" look. When the tablets are dry, they can be lightly sanded to lighten their appearance.

4 Roll a sheet of polymer clay to a thickness of ¼ in. Cut out a falcon shape. Make a template first if desired. Insert a hook into the falcon's head and bake. Press some of the canes made in step 1 into triangular shapes and cut off slices to make the falcon's feathers. Press down the slices firmly, then bake. When the clay has cooled, build up a feather pattern on the other side of the falcon and bake again.

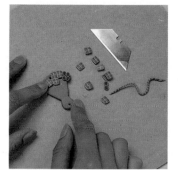

5 Make the papyrus piece in the same way, using square-section slices of cane to build up the pattern. Make a small hole in the top and bottom before baking.

6 Take four long lengths of gold thread and thread the glass beads onto them, alternating the shapes. Tie one end of the threads to the top of each of the tablets. Take 12 short lengths of thread and thread with glass and polymer clay beads. Attach to the bases of the tablets. Tie the tablets to the arms of the mobile crosspiece. Link the falcon and papyrus piece together with thread and attach to the center of the crosspiece with another length of thread.

Polymer clay is a material which is easy to model and can be baked in a domestic oven. Rolled into colored canes and sliced, it can also be used to create richly intricate patterns. (Deborah Alexander)

Sublime abstractions

mobiles featuring abstract shapes

The very first mobiles, created by Alexander Calder in the 1930s, were abstract in form. Usually typified by strong, graphic shapes that intrigue the eye, the shadows that abstract mobiles create when lit are just as fascinating. They can be as simple or complex as you wish, and the ideas included here range from simple twist-outs made from cut and scored cardboard to intricate abstract faces inspired by the work of famous artists.

Artists' gallery

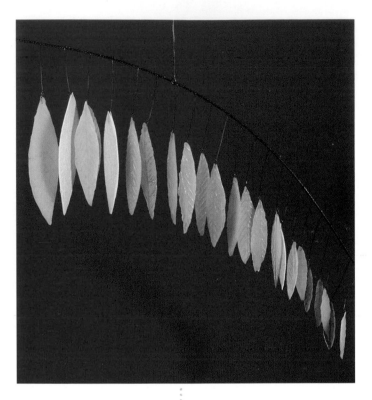

Leaf mobile

These stylized leaves are made from molded recycled glass and descend in size to make a very beautiful mobile. (Heidi Westgate)

Bell curtain

This Andean bell curtain combines clay beads and bells in a pleasing geometric arrangement. (People and Planet)

Leaf hanging

*Here leaves are suspended
in strands using recycled glass,
copper and leather thongs to
form a decorative wall hanging.
(Heidi Westgate)*

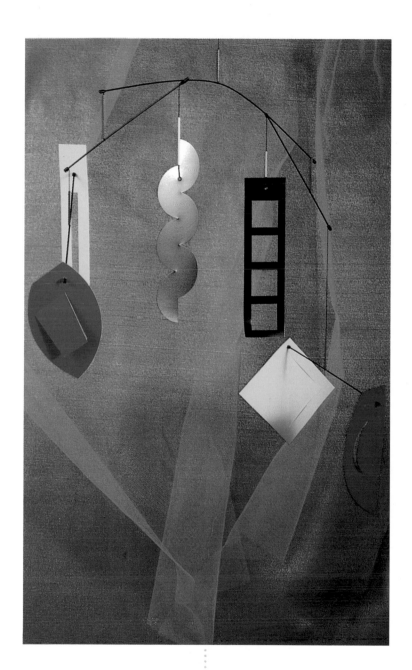

Geometric

*Geometric shapes hang
from the frame in an unpredictable
way to create constantly
changing abstract patterns.
(Louise Slater)*

Instant inspiration

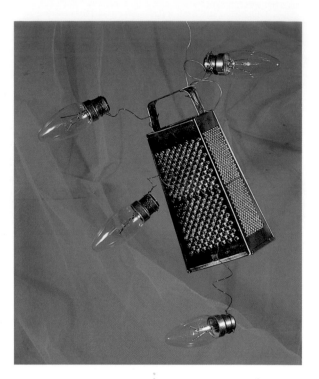

Light effects

*Attach small light bulbs to
a metal grater with wire for a
surprising and alternative mobile.*

Abstract curves

*Suspend architect's curve rulers
to make an elegant mobile that is
best positioned near a light
source so that it casts shadows.*

Rustic pegs

*Attach lengths of wire to a
stick and clip wooden pegs onto
each wire. Twist the pegs to
stick out at different angles.*

Nuts and bolts

*Hang copper plumbing pipe,
washers and chains from a piece
of driftwood to create a
mobile of contrasting textures
and materials.*

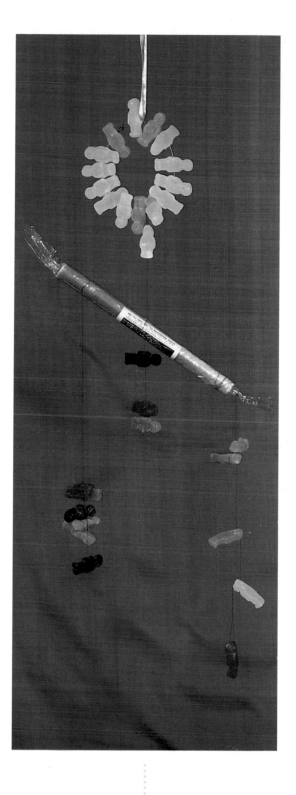

Candy shapes

*A stick of rock makes an
excellent crossbar from which to
hang a collection of delicious
candies. To preserve this mobile,
coat the candies in clear varnish.*

Stabile face

Τhis mobile works by balancing on a pivot point rather than hanging down. It was inspired by the work of the first mobile maker, Alexander Calder.

tools and materials

galvanized wire | *snub-nosed pliers* | *small pieces of* ¹⁄₈ *in cast acrylic* | *coping saw* | *drill* | *sandpaper* | *small block of florist's foam* | *small bottle* | *white glue* |

The "stabile" was the precursor of the mobile. This face is made from drilled cast acrylic pieces and twisted wire. (Labeena Ishaque)

1 Curve and twist the wire into a face shape, making three small loops at the top of the head. Twist the end pieces together to form the neck.

2 Using snub-nosed pliers, bend four hooks of varying lengths from which to hang the features.

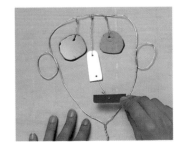

3 From the cast acrylic and using the coping saw, cut two circles for the eyes and two rectangles for the nose and mouth. Drill a hole at the top of the mouth and eyes, and at the top and bottom of the nose. Sand down all the edges.

4 Hang the facial features from the loops at the top of the head, using the hooks made in step 2. Place some florist's foam into the neck of the small bottle and push the stabile into the foam. Fix in place with white glue, if necessary.

Abstract face 1

This mobile is inspired by the current work of David Hockney, who has turned away from superrealism to a more abstract form of expression.

tools and materials

paper | pencil | scissors | modeling clay | rolling pin | craft knife | skewer | sandpaper | acrylic paints | paintbrushes | clear varnish | string |

1 Copy the template from the back of the book onto paper and cut out the component parts.

2 Soften the modeling clay by rolling it into a ball in your hands. Then roll out the clay with a rolling pin to a thickness of approximately 3/16 in.

3 Place the template pieces on the clay and cut out the shapes with the craft knife. Using a skewer, make holes where indicated on the template. Allow the modeling clay to dry according to the manufacturer's instructions.

4 When dry, sand the edges of each piece and decorate with acrylic paints in your chosen colors. Varnish with clear varnish. Assemble the mobile by tying the pieces together with string.

Made from self-hardening clay, this weird and wonderful abstract mobile will cast intriguing shadows in a lit room. (Ofer Acoo)

Abstract face 2

This bizarre yet beautiful face is inspired by the work of Pablo Picasso. Each piece hangs from the one above to create movement and expression as in the human face.

tools and materials

modeling clay | *rolling pin* | *craft knife* | *thin galvanized wire* | *copper wire* | *wire cutters* | *snub-nosed pliers* | *acrylic paints* | *paintbrushes* |

1 Using the template at the back of the book as a guide, cut out the shapes from modeling clay with a craft knife. Model the shapes in your hands to make three-dimensional features.

2 To make the right eye, skewer together the eyebrow shape and an eyeball with thin wire. Using snub-nosed pliers, curl a piece of copper wire and press into the eyebrow.

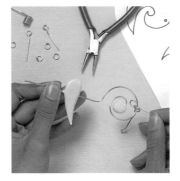

3 To make the left eye, curl copper wire into an intricate question mark shape and press an eyeball onto the inner end. Thread the eyebrow piece onto the long end. Cut four short lengths of copper wire. Make a loop at both ends of one of the pieces and at one end of the other three. Hook the loops onto the question mark shape. Make several small copper wire circles and attach them to the eye piece to make eyelashes.

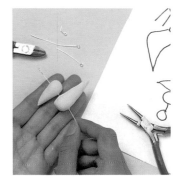

4 Thread thin wire through all the features while the modeling clay is still pliable. Make a hook at one end of each piece of wire before inserting into the clay. When the clay has set, form a hook at the other end of each piece of wire. Using wire, make holes in the main hanger piece as shown on the template.

5 Paint the features with acrylic paints, using your chosen colors.

6 When dry, assemble the face by hooking all the pieces together.

The separate elements of an abstract face readily lend themselves to the mobile form. The wires play as important a part in the final appearance of the structure as do the clay features. (Ofer Acoo)

Partridge in a pear tree

A truly beautiful mobile which catches the light as it moves. This is a special project and requires some experience in the use of glass and solder.

tools and materials

glass cutter | metal ruler | picture glass | $^1/_{16}$ in copper foil tape | piece of wood | $^1/_{16}$ in copper wire | wire cutters | snub- and flat-nosed pliers | soldering iron | safety flux | 50/50 tin/lead solder | 4 reduction rings | sandpaper | mineral spirits | paper | pencil | contour paste | glass paints | paintbrushes | ribbons | needle and thread | jump rings | swivel |

1 Using a glass cutter and metal ruler, cut 15 equilateral triangles and a diamond shape from the picture glass. If you don't feel confident about cutting the glass, most glass stores will be able to help.

Press copper foil tape along the edges of each piece of glass, overlapping the place where you started. Press the tape down firmly with a piece of wood.

2 To make the hangers, cut 2 in lengths of copper wire. Bend each into a "U" shape using snub-nosed pliers. Grip one side of the "U" with a pair of flat-nosed pliers about halfway down its length and bend it at a right angle. Repeat on the other side. Grip the loop of the "U" with the snub-nosed pliers and bend both sides upwards so that the hanger looks like an inverted keyhole.

From the copper wire, cut five branches 6 in long, five 5 in long and five 3 in long. Cut two bars to make the central hanging point, one 9 in long and one 6 in long.

3 Heat the soldering iron. Brush the copper-taped edges of a glass shape with flux. Melt a bead of solder on the iron, turn the iron on its side and draw it down each edge of the glass, coating the copper tape. Repeat with each piece of glass.

Pick up a hanger using pliers. Brush it with flux and draw it through a bead of molten solder. Grip the other end and repeat to "tin" it completely. Repeat with all the hangers and branches.

Position a hanger on the corner of a glass shape. Brush lightly with flux and touch the iron, with solder, to each end of the hanger, to secure. Repeat with the remaining glass shapes.

4 Rub down the upper side of two of the reduction rings and all of the branches with sandpaper, then wipe them with mineral spirits to degrease them. On a piece of paper, draw ten radiating lines 36 degrees apart. Put a reduction ring in the center and brush it with flux. Apply a dab of solder where each branch will be fixed. Position alternate 6 in and 5 in branches around the ring. Reflux and melt the branches into position. Solder the five 3 in branches onto the other ring in the same way (they will be 72 degrees apart). Using snub-nosed pliers, bend a loop at the end of each branch.

5 Draw your chosen designs for the glass pieces onto paper. Practice drawing the letter "S" on a piece of spare glass. Wash the glass shapes, then use contour paste to trace the raised outlines onto the glass. Leave to dry for at least two hours before you start painting.

Fill in the details of the designs with glass paint. Glass paint sets as soon as you apply it, so it is important to work quickly. Lift up the glass to the light, keeping it horizontal, to check your work and retouch it as necessary.

6 Cut ten ribbons 10 in long and five ribbons 5 in long. Fold in the ends about 1 in and tie a knot to form a loop. Sew the ribbons around the swivels. Push the reduction rings over the soldered rings. Assemble the glass shapes and ribbons and attach the jump rings and swivel for hanging.

The skills required for this project make it one of the most demanding in the book, but the finished mobile is well worth the effort. (Michael Ball)

Organgy curlicues

Let your imagination run absolutely free. Rolls of iridescent silks and satins, wreathed in luxurious sheer organdy, form an original and very feminine abstract mobile.

tools and materials

1 yd white cotton-covered wire | wire cutters | flat-nosed pliers | silk or satin scraps in toning shades | ivory silk organdy scraps | needle and thread | safety pin | 45 in fine copper wire | white cotton thread |

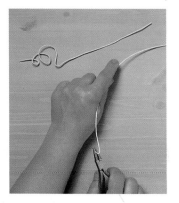 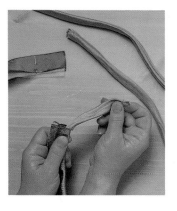  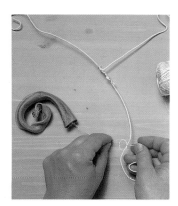

1 To make the frame, cut the cotton-covered wire into two pieces, one 22 in and one 14 in long. Use flat-nosed pliers to bend one end of the short wire to make a spiral and to curve each end of the long wire into a hook. Twist the unspiralled end of the short piece around the center of the long wire.

2 To make the curlicues, cut out three strips of silk or satin on the bias, one measuring 2½ × 20 in, one 2½ × 14 in and one 2½ × 8 in. Cut out three strips of organdy to the same measurements. Pair each silk strip with a piece of organdy. Fold each pair in half lengthwise so that the organdy is on the inside. Sew along the long edge. Using a safety pin, pull the organdy onto the outside.

3 Cut three pieces of copper wire slightly longer than the fabric strips and thread one piece through each curlicue. Twist one end of the wire around the end of the curlicue, tucking the raw edge inside first. Curve the tube into a spiral shape. Twist the other end of the wire to form a hook, tucking the raw edges of the fabric in as before.

4 Tie the curlicues to the frame with lengths of cotton thread.

Try varying the choice of fabric, the length of the wired tubes and the shapes formed from them to create your own designs.
(Karen Triffitt)

Pink twist-outs

This crisp, geometric mobile is formed by simply scoring and cutting cardboard within a square.

tools and materials

medium-weight cardboard, white on one side and pink on the other | pencil | ruler | craft knife | eraser | hole punch | cord or thread |

1 Cut a square of cardboard 7 × 7 in. Draw two diagonals lightly across the cardboard. Draw two 90-degree "V" shapes as shown. Note that one is closer to the edge of the cardboard.

2 Draw another pair of "V"s inside the first on the second diagonal. Draw a third pair of "V"s on the first diagonal.

3 Draw a final pair of "V"s on the second diagonal. If there is space, continue to fill the cardboard.

4 Carefully cut along the "V"s with a craft knife. Erase the pencil lines and punch a hole in one corner of the shape.

5 With the cardboard still flat, score short lines between the ends of the "V"s where you will fold the cardboard. Do this by turning the craft knife blade upside-down and carefully running it along the edge of a ruler.

6 Fold the cardboard along the scored lines and pull out to form a series of twisted square shapes positioned within each other.

7 Thread cord or thread through the punched hole for hanging. If desired, make a second twist-out and suspend it from the first.

Each made from a single piece of two-colored cardboard, the twisted squares demonstrate that stunning mobiles can be made from the simplest of materials.
(Paul Jackson)

Airborne seashores

mobiles with a sea-life theme

The sea and the lifeforms within it are enduringly popular images, associated as they often are with gentle, rhythmic movements that engender a sense of peace and well-being. The artists featured in this chapter have chosen a diverse range of sea creatures to depict – whales, crabs, seahorses, tropical fish, an octopus – and the materials and techniques used to create them are just as varied. Perfect for bathrooms and bedrooms: lie back and relax as you watch them gently revolve.

Artists' gallery

Ocean depths

*The shapes represent a shark,
lobster, starfish and seahorse.
(Al Brown/Papier Marché)*

Happy mermaid

*The mythical figure of the
mermaid is amusingly portrayed
here with her school of
vibrant tropical fish.
(Jim Edminston/Lucky Parrot)*

Tropical fish

*The bright silhouettes look
great against a plain background.
(Louise Slater)*

Aquarium

*These realistic angel fish
provide an instant aquarium with
none of the maintenance chores.
(7 & 7 Interiors)*

Sky fish

*Small papier-mâché fish
are hung from a star-shape
support made from bamboo
sticks tied together.
(Sara Drake)*

Seascape

*A hungry papier-mâché sea
bird hovers over a submerged fish.
(James Dean)*

Instant inspiration

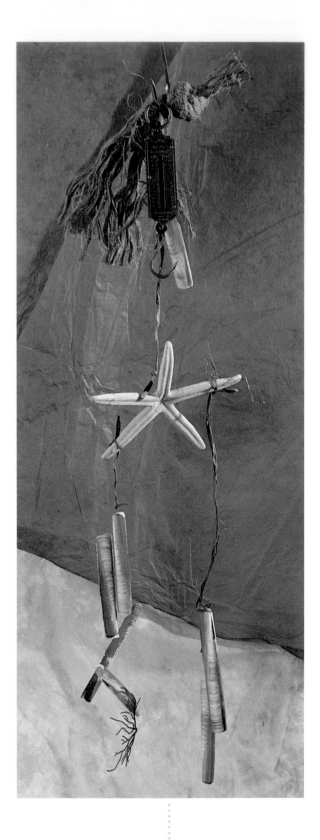

Deep blue sea

*Cover a coat-hanger in blue
crêpe or tissue paper to represent
the sea. Hang plastic toy
dolphins, turtles and other sea
creatures below the hanger.*

Beachcomber

*Make an unusual windchime
by hanging cuttlefish bones from a
beached starfish and hang it
in a doorway or by a window.*

Silver fish

*Suspend fish-shaped gelatin
molds from a shell-shaped mold
to make a seashore mobile
for the kitchen.*

Shore finds

*Hang shells and scraps of
fishing net from a scallop shell to
evoke a small fishing port.*

Octopus's garden

This is an inexpensive and easy way to make a mobile – brightly colored paper is simply torn and stuck together to form the bold sea creatures.

tools and materials

thin cardboard | *scissors* | *papers, brightly colored on one side* | *pencil* | *white glue* | *hole punch* | *thread* |

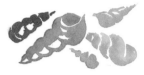

1 Cut out two identical octopus shapes from cardboard, using the template at the back of the book, and eight simple fish, squid and starfish shapes in varying sizes to your own design.

2 Fold the paper so that the colored side is innermost. Draw around each of the cardboard shapes. Tear out each shape, slightly outside the pencil outline. As you have folded the paper, you will tear out two copies of each shape.

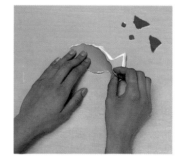

3 Glue the paper onto both sides of each cardboard shape. Using contrasting colors, tear out eyes, fins, tails and scales. Glue them into position.

4 Cut a slot in each of the octopus shapes, one to halfway down from the top of the head and the other to halfway up from the bottom of the body. Punch a hole at the end of each octopus arm and two holes in each head piece. Punch a hole at the top edge of each sea creature.

5 Slot together the two octopus pieces.

6 Use thread to hang the sea creatures from the octopus's arms. Tie thread to the top of the octopus's head for hanging.

Simply made from colored paper, the friendly octopus and fish will delight children and brighten up a bedroom or bathroom. (Labeena Ishaque)

Under the sea

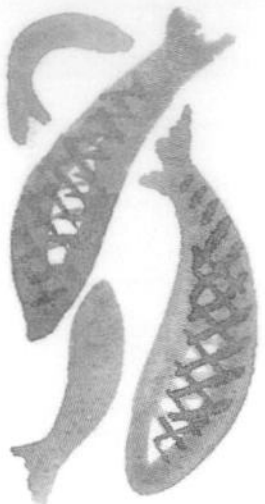

Rich shades of turquoise, coral and blue, edged in gold, are used to make these larger-than-life sea creatures.

tools and materials

3 blocks of florist's foam | craft knife | cardboard | scissors | white glue | wallpaper paste | newspaper | small brass curtain rings | masking tape | string | white latex | paintbrushes | acrylic paints | 6 glass nuggets | gold paint | 2 round beads | gloss varnish | galvanized wire | fishing line |

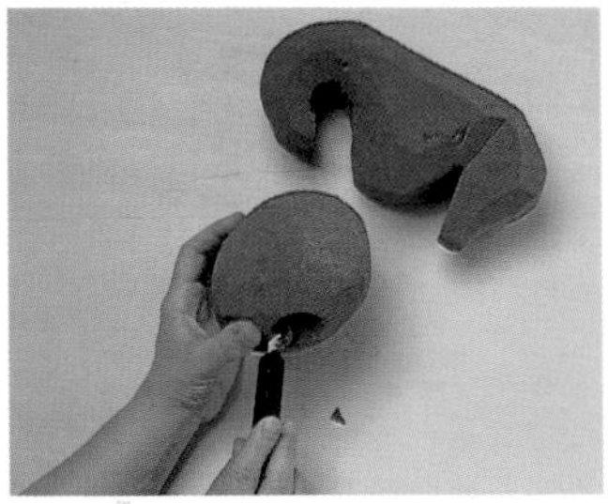

1 Carve one of the florist's foam blocks into a rough seahorse shape. Cut the remaining two blocks in half to create four pieces for the fishes. Carve off the corners of all four pieces to make oval shapes. At one end of each block, carve out a mouth shape.

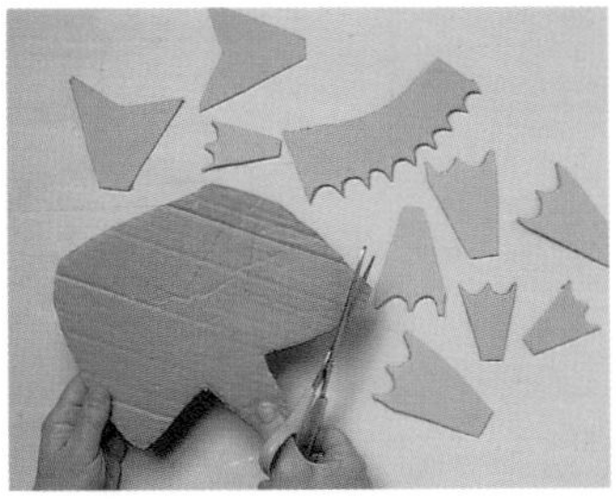

2 Use the templates at the back of the book to cut out shapes from the cardboard. Cut out two side fins and one underside fin, one dorsal fin and one tail for each fish. Cut out a back fin, then two side fins and a headpiece for the seahorse. Cut out a starfish shape.

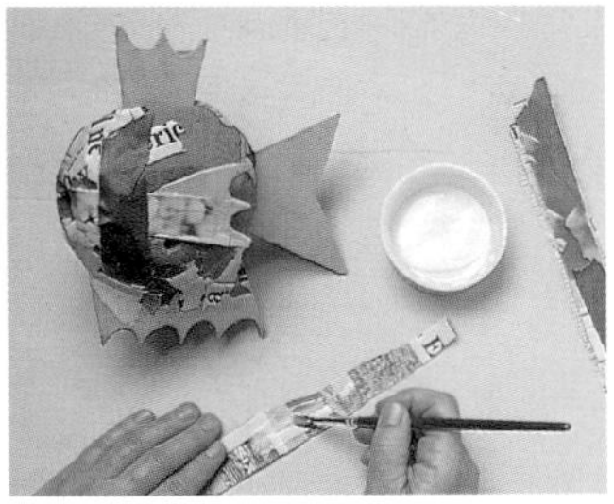

3 Cut slots in the foam blocks and insert the fins, tails and headpiece. Glue them in place. Using wallpaper paste, cover the fishes and seahorse in several layers of newspaper strips. Allow them to dry.

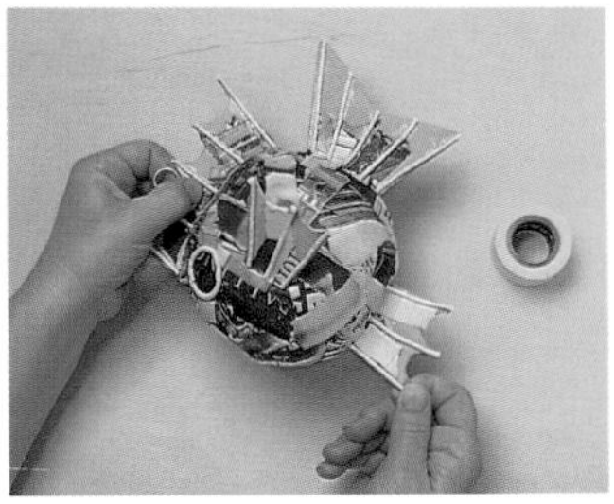

4 Tape a brass ring into the central curve of each fish's dorsal fin and into the first curve of the seahorse's back fin. Tape a ring onto the end of a starfish arm and another onto the body directly opposite. Glue lengths of string along the fins and tails of the fishes and seahorse and around the eyes to give definition to the sea creatures' features.

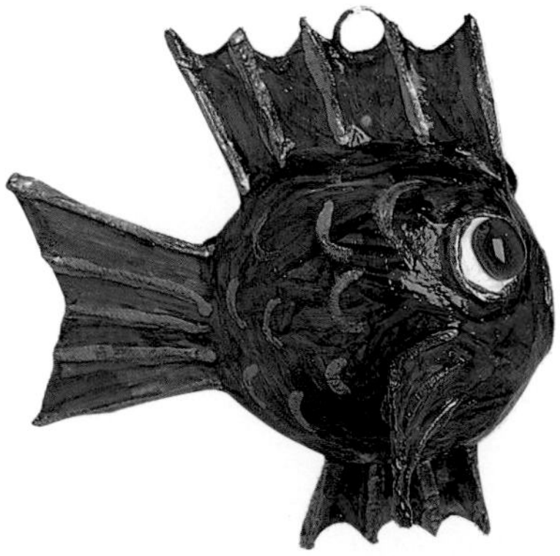

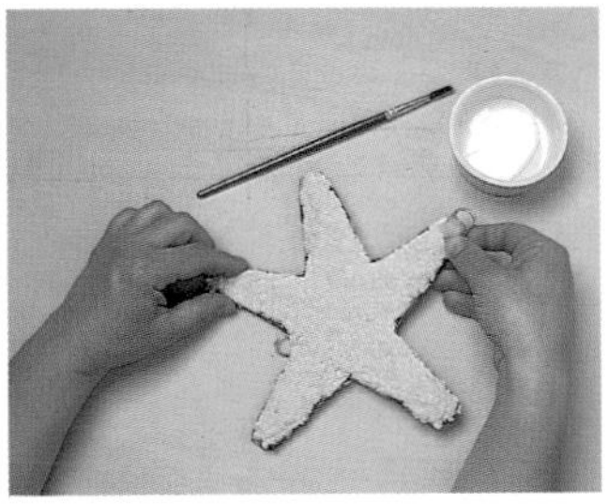

5 Cover the starfish in paper pulp and allow to dry. Cover the fishes, starfish and seahorse with more layers of pasted newspaper strips. Carefully cover the joins of the brass rings. Allow the pieces to dry.

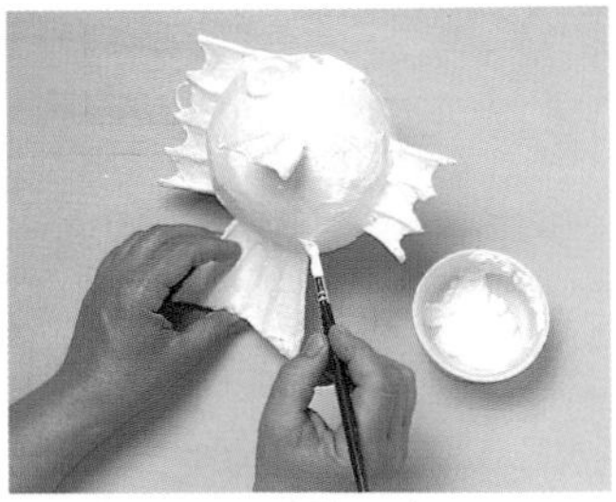

6 Paint all the shapes with white latex paint. Allow to dry.

7 Paint the fishes blue with orange mouths. Leave the eyes white and glue on the glass nuggets. Paint the starfish in shades of orange and the seahorse blue-green. Paint the elevated details made by the string in gold. Paint around the eyes in gold. Stick the beads onto the seahorse's face for eyes. Allow the paint to dry and then apply varnish to all the sea creatures.

8 Join two 16 in lengths of wire in the center to make a crosspiece. Attach 8 in lengths of fishing line to the ends of the crosspiece and tie the end of each line to the brass ring on each fish. Attach a longer length of fishing line to the center of the crosspiece and suspend the seahorse from this. Attach a shorter length of fishing line to the crosspiece and tie to the ring on the starfish body. Tie a length of line to the ring on the starfish arm for hanging the mobile.

The glossy blues, greens and oranges of the papier-mâché sea creatures eloquently capture the atmosphere of ocean depths.
(Bridget Hinge)

Whale and crabs

A cheerful whale swims close to the ocean's surface, keeping a beady eye on the antics of the crabs lurking in the depths below.

tools and materials

pencil | thin colored cardboard | craft knife and/or scissors | ruler | pin | double-sided sticky tape | coping saw | 2 × 12 in lengths of ¼ × ¼ in square-section dowel | wood glue | 2 large moving eyes | white glue | 2 yd narrow white ribbon or piping cord | 16 small moving eyes | fishing line |

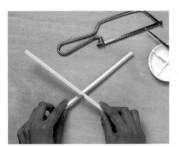
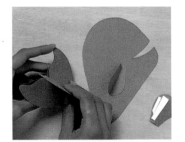

1 Use the templates at the back of the book to trace and cut out all the pieces from colored cardboard. Score along the dotted lines, make pinholes where indicated and stick double-sided sticky tape in the shaded areas.

2 With a coping saw, cut a rabbet in the center of each piece of dowel and glue together to form a cross.

3 To make the whale, first stick the taped half of each tail section onto either side of the main body tail area. Now stick a fin to each side of the body and secure the large eyes to either side of the head with white glue. Allow to dry completely.

4 To make the crabs, tie the three arm sections together with white ribbon or cord and attach to either side of the body. Glue the small eyes to the front and back of each body.

Opposite page:
Children will love helping to make
this colorful cardboard mobile.
(Lisa Gilchrist)

5 To make the sand, mark four equally spaced points on the inside

of each of the yellow strips of cardboard. Make a pinhole at each point. Curve each strip into a ring and secure firmly. Make the crosses with the smaller yellow strips of cardboard and stick the ends to the points you have marked inside the rings. Make the blue and turquoise wave pieces in the same way.

6 To make the seaweed, curve and stick the four green strips to form rings. Make a large white wave ring in the same way. There is no need to add crosspieces to these sections as they will be supported.

7 Insert a green seaweed ring within each sand ring. Tie a 4 in length of fishing line to each of the pinholes in the sand. Tie the four ends together and tie each sand piece to the base of a crab. Tie a crab to each of the four holes in the blue wave. Insert the turquoise and white rings inside the blue wave. Tie a 12 in length of fishing line to each of the pinholes in the blue wave. Tie the ends together and attach to the bottom of the whale. Attach fishing line to the whale's head and tail. Using double-sided sticky tape, stick water droplets onto either side of the line above the whale's head. Tie the threads to the wooden crosspiece.

Fish and crocodile

Inspired by the sea but
also including flowers and stars,
not to mention a wandering
crocodile, this mobile is made
from plywood.

tools and materials

pencil | 3/16 in plywood | coping saw | drill |
fine-grade sandpaper | paintbrushes | white latex paint |
acrylic paints | gold paint | gloss varnish | wood glue |
fishing line |

Opposite page:
The most basic woodwork
skills are all that are required in
the construction of this
sea-inspired mobile. (Jill Hancock)

1 Using the templates at
the back of the book,
draw the hanging motifs and
the hanging bars on the
plywood. Cut them out with a
coping saw.

2 Drill small holes in the
pieces as shown on the
templates. Sand down the
edges with fine-grade
sandpaper until smooth.

3 Apply two coats of
white latex paint to the
shapes. Allow to dry, then
lightly sand the shapes with
fine-grade sandpaper
between coats.

4 Paint the shapes with
acrylic paints and add
details with gold paint. Finish
with a coat of gloss varnish.
Glue the crossbar together.
Tie the shapes to the crossbar
with fishing line.

Suspend
the everyday

mobiles for the kitchen

Kitchens are often places where you will
see objects hanging from the walls or ceiling,
whether pots and pans, cooking utensils,
herbs or flowers for drying, or strings of onions
and garlic. This chapter includes some fun
ideas for creating innovative kitchen mobiles,
both using traditional kitchen materials and
mimicking objects you would find there.

Artists' gallery

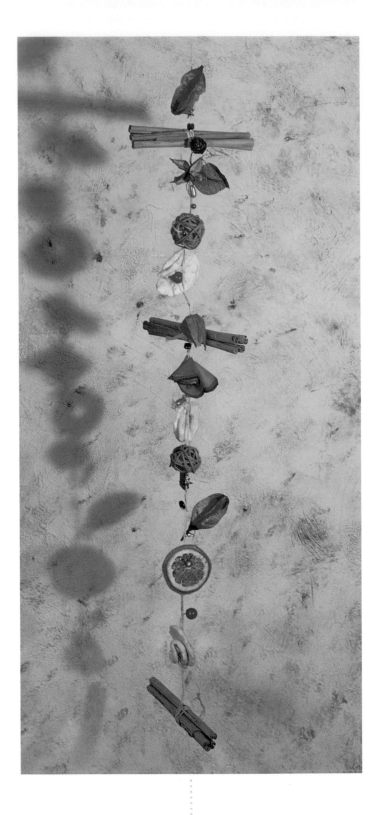

Egg basket

*Pastry cutters of a man
and a woman are suspended
from a wire hen basket
bound with gingham.
(Author's collection)*

Simply delicious

*This selection of seed pods,
orange slices, cinnamon sticks and
apple rings is a warm orange
in color and has a delicious smell.
(Author's collection)*

Aromatic herbs

*There are many ways of
making decorative mobiles with
dried herbs and foods. This
one uses closely packed bay leaves
suspended on a gingham ribbon.
(Shaker shop)*

All in a line

*The hen is a popular image for
kitchenware ranging from eggcups
to cookie jars. This lively mobile
is a string of fabric roosting hens.
(7 & 7 Interiors)*

Instant inspiration

Tableware

*Use pliers to twist fork prongs
into bizarre shapes and hang from
an old toast rack to make an
eccentrically picturesque mobile.*

Well-seasoned

*Fill glass salt and pepper
pots with colored water and hang
from a metal steamer to create a
mobile in the form of a chandelier.*

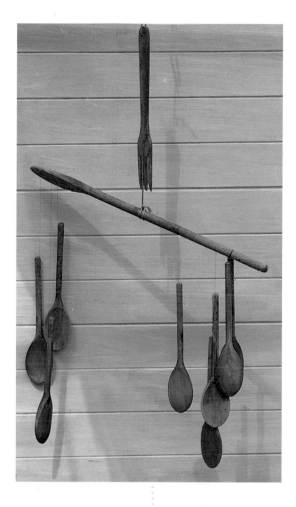

Stir crazy

*Paint wooden spoons in
bright colors and drill a hole in
the end of each. Suspend
them from a painted wooden fork
to make a cheerful and
inexpensive kitchen decoration.*

Hot and spicy

*Fill a mesh basket with bright
red chili peppers and hang more
peppers around the edges.
Attach the basket to a tea strainer
and add a loop for hanging.*

Iced cookies

In Germany these cookies are called *lebkuchen* and are often sold at street fairs. The recipe makes quite a large quantity of cookies, so you can use them to make this pretty kitchen mobile with plenty left over for the family to sample.

cookie dough (see recipe) | *rolling pin* | *cookie cutters* | *skewer* | *baking sheet* | *wire rack* | *icing mixture (see recipe)* | *piping bag fitted with a small, plain nozzle* | *large wooden spoon* | *drill* | *gingham ribbon* | *red ribbon* | *large needle* |

Recipe

cookie dough

1/2 cup clear honey

1 cup brown sugar

2 tbsp butter

grated rind and juice of 1/2 lemon

1 egg

2 cups flour

1 tsp baking powder

1/2 tsp ground cinnamon

1/2 tsp ground cloves

1/4 tsp ground nutmeg

1 tsp ground ginger

pinch salt

icing

2 tbsp egg white

1/2 cup confectioner's sugar

For the cookie dough, place the honey, sugar and butter in a small saucepan and heat gently until the butter has melted and the sugar has dissolved. Allow the mixture to cool slightly. Stir in the lemon rind and juice, then beat in the egg. Sift the dry ingredients into a bowl, then beat about a third into the melted mixture. Work in the remainder of the dry ingredients.

For the icing, lightly whisk the egg white with a fork, then sift and stir in the confectioner's sugar. Mix until smooth.

1 On a lightly floured surface, knead the cookie dough until smooth. Roll out to a 1/4 in thickness and cut out shapes with the cookie cutters. Make a hole at the top of each cookie with a skewer and bake on a greased baking sheet at 325°F for 20 minutes. Let cool slightly, then transfer to a wire rack and allow to cool completely.

2 Fill the piping bag with icing and decorate the cookies with iced patterns.

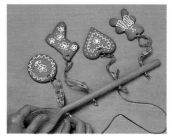

4 Thread the gingham ribbon through the holes in the cookies and hang from the wooden spoon. Thread the ends of the red ribbon through two of the holes in the spoon, knot and use to hang the mobile.

3 Drill four holes along the handle of the wooden spoon.

The wooden spoon reflects the baking theme of this edible mobile.
(Dorothy Wood)

Colander and vegetables

The old-fashioned colander and bright fresh vegetables are in fact made from papier-mâché!

tools and materials

large bowl | petroleum jelly | newspaper | wallpaper paste | galvanized wire | wire cutters | fine-grade sandpaper | white latex paint | paintbrushes | acrylic paints | masking tape | crêpe paper | tissue paper | twine | white glue | clear varnish | needle and thread |

1 Cover the outside of a colander-sized bowl with petroleum jelly. Cover the bowl in layers of newspaper strips. Start by sticking them with water to avoid them sticking to the mold, then use wallpaper paste. Allow the papier-mâché to dry.

2 Remove the shape from the mold and trim the edge. Add more papier-mâché to neaten the edge if necessary. Once dry, push two pieces of curved wire into the rim to make handles. Wrap paper strips around the handles and paste.

3 When dry, gently sand down the surface of the colander shape, and apply a coat of white latex. With blue paint, make patterns for the "holes" on both sides of the colander shape, and paint the rim and handles.

4 Crumple pieces of newspaper to make a carrot, a corn cob, a pepper, a celery head and two tomatoes. Bind the shapes with masking tape, then cover them as evenly as possible with layers of papier-mâché. Allow to dry.

5 Gently sand down the shapes and apply a coat of white latex. Paint the vegetables with acrylic paints, adding texture by splattering, rubbing and sanding each shape.

6 Add crêpe paper and colored tissue paper to represent leaves. Glue unravelled twine onto the corn cob to represent the husk. Varnish the vegetables if desired.

7 Tie colored thread of varying lengths to the vegetable stems. Pass the other ends of the threads through the colander for hanging. Make adjustments to achieve the right balance.

The hanging vegetables give the appearance of tumbling from the colander after having been washed. (Melanie Williams)

Nature's bounty

This pretty mobile is also a practical way of hanging dried fruits, seeds and spices in the kitchen. As new produce comes into season, it can be added to your mobile.

tools and materials

chicken wire | wire cutters | moss | dried fruits and vegetables: for example, lemons, peppers, chilies | fine string or buttonhole thread | large needle | cinnamon sticks | dried bay leaves |

1 Cut the chicken wire and roll into a thick tube shape. Stuff the wire tube with the moss.

2 Sew the dried fruit and the peppers together with fine string to the length required.

3 Thread the chilies onto a length of string. Make bundles of cinnamon sticks and tie onto a length of thread.

4 Tuck bay leaves into the moss. Attach the lengths of fruit and vegetables to the moss log and add a loop for hanging.

Opposite page:
Ready-made decorations of natural materials are very popular. Making your own is much less expensive and more satisfying than purchasing them.
(Dorothy Wood)

Teatime

This easy-to-make mobile, using decoupage, has a lovely traditional look – a must for committed tea drinkers.

tools and materials

white cardboard | colored cardboard | teacup images from gift-wrap or magazine | scissors | thread | white glue | needle |

Opposite page:
Shapes cut from wrapping paper make interesting mobile pieces when teamed with a suitable frame. The polka-dotted teapot is just right for these printed teacups. (Josephine Whitfield)

1 Using the template at the back of the book, cut out two teapots from the white cardboard and lots of dots from the colored cardboard. Cut out the teacups.

2 Sandwich the teacups together in pairs so that the images face outwards. Glue them together with a length of thread held in between for hanging.

3 Using a needle and thread, attach the teacups to the bottom of one of the teapot shapes. Glue the two teapots together.

4 Glue the dots onto either side of the teapot and, with a needle, attach thread to the top for hanging.

Floating enchantments

mobiles for romantics

For lovers everywhere, celebrate your

passion with a mobile suspended above the

bed or hanging over a lowlit table for two.

Hearts – the enduring emblem of love – feature

in most of the ideas you will find here,

from a Scandinavian raffia wreath and a bridal

"garter" in frothy lace and silks, to a

kissing couple sculpted from wire and a

romantic couple made of vibrantly painted

papier-mâché.

Artists' gallery

Love hearts

*A pair of intertwined hearts
is a traditional romantic symbol
representing the two
hearts beating as one.
(7 & 7 Interiors)*

Bouquet

*Another popular visual
image when it comes to romance
is flowers. These attractive
cascading ceramic flowers come
from South America.
(People and Planet)*

Shaker style

Padded gingham hearts,
strung on a single line, make a
wonderful folk-art decoration.
(Shaker shop)

Heavenly choir

The romantic golden angels
are made from tassels of string.
They have been hung around
a ring on increasing lengths of
thread to form a spiral.
(People and Planet)

Instant inspiration

Scented evenings

*Romance can often be
the evocation of perfumes from the
past. Cloves and oranges
are deliciously fragrant, without
being cloying.*

Lace fantasy

*Hang wedding-cake horseshoes
and lacy handkerchiefs from
a crossed wire frame to make a
romantic keepsake.*

Loving memories

*Cut pictures, postcards and
photos into heart shapes and hang
them from a gilt frame as a
reminder of a beloved one or
of a romantic holiday.*

Bridal ring

*For a lasting memento of
your wedding day, dry your bouquet
and hang the flowers around
a ring. Tie with ribbon at the top.*

Romantic couple

Made from highly decorated padded papier-mâché, this mobile would make a wonderful emblem of love to hang above your bed.

tools and materials

cardboard | craft knife | newspaper | masking tape | galvanized wire | wire cutters | snub-nosed pliers | wallpaper paste | small hooks | epoxy resin glue | mirror glass | hammer | plastic body filler | white glue | white acrylic primer | acrylic paints | paintbrushes | gold paint | clear varnish | jump rings | picture hanging wire |

1 Using the templates at the back of the book, cut out the hearts, human figures, the heart wings, the bird and the teardrops from cardboard. Crumple small pieces of newspaper and tape them to each shape to create the form. Leave the wings and the bird's tail uncovered. Make a slit either side of the heart shape, insert the wings and tape securely in place.

2 Using snub-nosed pliers, coil and bend two lengths of wire for the figure support and a length of wire for the bird's feet, following the templates at the back of the book. Tape the wire shapes to small pieces of cardboard. Bend and coil the other wire shapes, following the templates. Cut a slit at the base of the winged heart and bird, then insert the small pieces of cardboard and tape them securely in place.

3 Cover all the pieces in several layers of newspaper and wallpaper paste. Allow to dry. Screw in the small hooks where needed, securing them with epoxy resin glue.

4 Break the mirror glass by placing it between several layers of newspaper and hitting it gently with a hammer. Mix the plastic body filler according to the manufacturer's instructions. Apply to one side of each wing and carefully press in the pieces of mirror. Allow to dry and repeat on the other side of the wings. Coat all the pieces with white glue and then with acrylic primer. Don't paste or paint the mirror pieces.

5 Decorate the pieces with acrylic paints, adding details in gold paint. Coat the wire shapes with white glue, acrylic primer and gold paint. Allow them to dry completely.

6 Apply a coat of varnish to the wire pieces and three coats of varnish to the painted pieces. Assemble the mobile by joining the pieces together with jump rings. Suspend the mobile using picture hanging wire.

Protected by the heart above their heads and the bird of peace beneath their feet, how could this couple be anything other than loving? (Kim Rowley)

Scandinavian hearts

Braided raffia hearts hang from a pretty willow wreath. Beads and ribbons complete this traditional love gift.

tools and materials

red and natural raffia | *scissors* | *tapestry needle* | *fine cord* | *beads* | *willow wreath* | *red ribbon* | *strong glue or glue gun* |

1 Make large and small hearts from raffia. Braid together nine strands of raffia for the large hearts and six strands for the small hearts.

2 Cut off 8 in lengths of braid for the large hearts and 5½ in lengths for the small hearts. Bind the ends together securely with a length of raffia to form a loop. Darn in the loose end of raffia with a tapestry needle.

3 Turn the loop inside out and ease into a heart shape. Pinch the end to make a sharp point.

4 Thread the hearts onto lengths of fine cord, interspersing them with small groups of beads.

5 Bind the willow wreath with the red ribbon and secure with glue. Cut three 12 in lengths of ribbon and tie them to the wreath, taking care to space them evenly. Glue them into place and tie the ends together for hanging.

6 Attach the lengths of hearts and beads to the wreath by tying them onto willow twigs.

Opposite page: Red and white are traditional Scandinavian colors and make a bold statement. (Lucinda Ganderton)

Sealed with a kiss

Two stylized profiles constructed from gold-painted wire gaze into each other's eyes.

tools and materials

thin galvanized wire | *wire cutters* | *snub-nosed pliers* |

gold enamel paint | *paintbrush* |

What more potent symbol of love is there than a kiss? This wire mobile is best hung to dramatic effect in front of deep-colored fabric or curtains. (Labeena Ishaque)

1 Using the template at the back of the book as a guide, sculpt the wire with snub-nosed pliers to form two profiles.

2 Use the template to form the hooks and the heart with pliers.

3 Paint the wire pieces with gold enamel paint. Allow to dry.

4 Attach a hook to each of the profiles and the heart. Position so that the profiles face each other and the heart hangs centrally. Twist together the wire hooks and bend into a hook at the top for hanging.

Bridal hearts

Ivory-white silk, lace and pearls combine to form this delicate and feminine decoration – a perfect gift for a bride.

tools and materials

13 in length of tubular foam | white fabric | needle and thread | plain and decorated lengths of pearls | 2 in wide lace | silk fabric scraps | batting | tiny seed pearls and beads | fabric roses | glass beads and hearts |

1 Cover the length of tubular foam in white fabric. Sew the ends together to form a ring.

2 Wrap a length of pearls around the ring and secure the ends with needle and thread. Wrap the lace around the ring between the pearls and sew down.

3 Cut out six hearts from silk. Pair the hearts and sew around the edges with right sides facing. Leave a small opening for the batting. Turn the right way out and stuff lightly. Slip stitch the opening. Decorate with tiny seed pearls, beads and a fabric rose. Sew the hearts onto lengths of pearls.

4 Sew the hanging hearts to the ring, interspersed with lengths of pearls decorated with glass beads and hearts. Sew glass beads and lace bows around the ring and attach four loops of lace for hanging.

An enduring reminder of a wedding day, this mobile is made from silk, pearls and lace. (Janet Bridge)

Scented chandelier

Hang this ethereal mobile above your dining table for a romantic meal.

tools and materials

wire cutters | thin galvanized wire | pliers | gold spray paint | scissors | acrylic paints | paintbrushes | thin cardboard | white glue | gold paint | masking tape | colored beads | metallic thread | silk fabric | needle and thread | lace | buttons | potpourri | ribbon |

1 Cut six pieces of wire to the same length. Using pliers, bend hooks at one end of the wires, then twist the wires together to about halfway down their length.

2 Bend out the other half of each wire to form the branches of the chandelier. Curl the ends upwards to form supports for the candle holders. Spray paint gold and allow to dry.

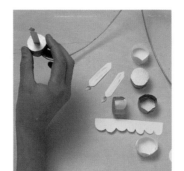

3 Cut out and paint six cardboard candles with flames. To make the candle holders, cut six circles of cardboard, leaving tabs around the edges. Cut six strips of cardboard as long as the diameter of each circle and cut scallops along one edge. Curve a strip around each circle, fold up the tabs and glue to the inside of the strip. Paint them gold. Cut a slit in the center of each circle and insert a candle. Attach a holder to the end of each chandelier branch with a ball of masking tape.

4 Thread assorted beads onto lengths of metallic thread. Tie knots in the thread to hold the beads in position. Then tie the threads to the chandelier.

5 Sew little pouches from silk. Decorate with lace, buttons and beads and fill with potpourri. Tie the tops with ribbon.

6 Sew a thread decorated with beads to the top of each purse and tie to the chandelier.

The Gothic extravagance of the chandelier is softened here by the addition of scented, lacy purses and strings of beads. (Melanie Williams)

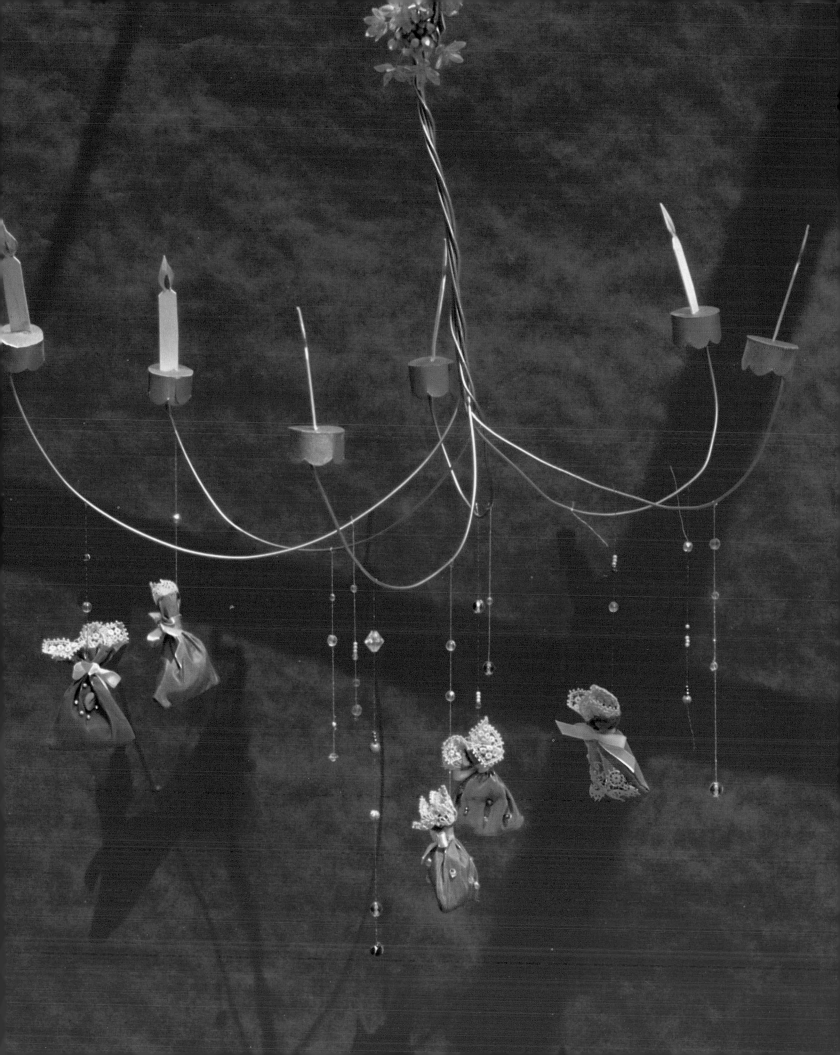

Carousel of hearts

A richly colored tent
covered in satin is used to suspend
a merry-go-round of padded
satin hearts.

tools and materials

galvanized wire | wire cutters | snub-nosed pliers | thin cardboard | scissors | pencil | masking tape | brightly colored satin fabric | double-sided sticky tape | needle and thread | batting | gold thread | gold enamel paint | paintbrush

*Opposite page:
Bring all the fun of the fair
into your home with this bright,
romantic carousel.
(Sameena Ishaque)*

1 Form two circles from the galvanized wire. Add four straight pieces of wire to one of the circles, spacing them evenly. Twist together the ends at the top to make the roof of the tent. Cut several short pieces of wire and then bend their ends into hooks.

2 Use the hooks to suspend the second circle from the roof. You may need to hang the structure up to do this.

3 Cut out a circle of thin cardboard. Draw a line from the center to the edge and cut along it. Curve the circle into a cone, position it over the top of the wire structure and secure with masking tape.

4 Cut a strip of cardboard to fit around the base of the tent and cover it with satin fabric, using double-sided sticky tape. Tape the strip in place on the wire structure.

5 Cut four triangles of satin to cover the cardboard cone. Stick them onto the cone with double-sided sticky tape, folding in a hem edge on each piece.

6 Cut five pairs of hearts from the fabric. Sew each pair together, right sides facing. Leave a small opening for batting. Turn the right way out and stuff. Slip stitch the opening. Sew gold thread at the top to hang. Tape the hanging threads to the bottom edge of the carousel.

7 Tuck in any raw edges of fabric on the tent. Paint the exposed wire at the top with gold enamel paint, line the seams with gold thread and add little bows of gold thread to decorate.

Entrancing cherubs

mobiles for babies

Mobiles are wonderful gifts for babies.
Their eyes are naturally drawn to bright colors
and simple shapes, and the gentle movements
will encourage focusing skills. All the
ideas featured here make use of soft, natural
materials to make them especially baby-
friendly. Choose from crocheted bees,
butterflies, teddy bears, lions and flowers.
When making mobiles for young infants,
make sure that they are well made and don't
use tiny items which might fall or be
pulled off and put in the mouth.

Artists' gallery

Bunny jumps

*These funny looking felt
bunnies with their pink ears make
a sweet baby mobile.
(People and Planet)*

Noddyland

*The Enid Blyton character
Noddy has been used to make a
charming mobile.
(Francis Trousselier/
David Rosenblatt)*

Two-by-two

*The ever-popular Noah's
ark, made from felt, is surrounded
by pairs of adorable animals.
(People and Planet)*

First alphabet

*These bright letters might
even encourage letter recognition!
(Louise Slater)*

Tumbling clowns

*These enchanting fabric clowns
are joined together by wire loops.
They twirl backwards and
forwards like real acrobats.
(Mrs Winter)*

Baby bears

*Everyone loves teddy bears and
these waistcoated ones, combined
with stars, make an appealing
mobile. (Jan Barber/Papier Marché)*

Instant inspiration

Little jugglers

*Tie softly tactile juggling
balls to a pole to make an unusual
alternative to a carriage
or crib mobile.*

Bathtime

*Take advantage of the
wide range of sponge shapes now
available to make a pretty
pastel mobile for baby's bathtime.*

Eye-catching

*Make a sparkling mobile
by threading small metallic
cupcake cases onto strings.
The mobile will turn in the air
and glitter in the light.*

Letter tracks

*Stick magnetic plastic letters
and numbers to sections of a child's
large-gauge railway track.
Hang extra letters and numbers
from the track.*

Friendly insects

Crocheted bees and ladybugs
gather around a colorful flower.
A baby will love to kick this
soft mobile with his or her feet.

tools and materials

double knitting cotton yarn in black, red, white, yellow, light blue,
orange, green, blue, pink and lime green | *E crochet hook* |
scissors | *batting* | *large-eyed needle* | *jewelry wire* |

abbreviations
st/s = stitch/es
ss = slip stitch
ch = chain stitch
sc = single crochet
dc = double crochet
hdc= half double crochet

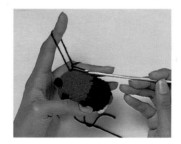

Ladybugs

Using black yarn and hook,
crochet two ladybugs as
follows:
3 ch, ss in 1st ch to form a
ring.
1st row: 1 ch, 5 sc into ring, ss
in first st at beginning of
round.
2nd row: 1 ch, 2 sc in each of
next 5 sts, ss in first st.
3rd row: 1 ch, 2 sc in each of
next 10 sts, ss in first st.
4th row: 1 ch, 1 sc in each of
next 20 sts, ss in first st.

5th, 6th, 7th rows: repeat 4th
row.
8th–13th rows: change to red
yarn and repeat 4th row. Take
a handful of batting and stuff
the ladybug.
14th row: 1 ch, * 1 sc in each
of next 3 sts, skip the
following st. Repeat from *
four more times, ss in first st
at beginning of round.
15th row: 1 ch, * 1 sc in each
of next 2 sts, skip the
following st. Repeat from *
four more times, ss in first st.
16th row: 1 ch, * 1 sc in first
st, skip the following st.
Repeat from * four more
times, ss in first st. With 1 yd
black yarn and a large-eyed
needle, embroider a central
line of chain stitch running
from the head along the back
of the ladybug.

Spots

Using black yarn and hook,
crochet two spots for each
ladybug as follows:
3 ch, ss in first ch to form a
ring. 1 ch, 5 sc into ring, ss in
first st at beginning of round.

Cast off, leaving 6–8 in of yarn
to stitch spots to each
ladybug on either side of the
chain-stitched line.

Eyes

Using white yarn and hook,
crochet two eyes for each
ladybug as follows:
3 ch, ss in first st to form a
ring. 1 ch, 4 sc into ring, ss in
first st at beginning of round.
Cast off, leaving
approximately a 6–8 in end of
yarn to stitch the eyes to the
ladybugs' heads.

Legs

Work six legs on each
ladybug as follows:
With a 2 yd length of black
yarn, cast on by drawing 2½–
3 in of yarn through the
ladybug's body at the first leg
position and form a chain. * 3
ch, 1 sc in second ch, 1 sc in
next ch. Cast off. Insert hook
at next leg position,
approximately ½ in away
from the first leg. Insert the
hook into the ladybug again,
as close to the end of yarn as

possible. Draw the yarn
through to form a chain.
Repeat from * until six legs
are made; sew in the ends.

Mouth

With a 16 in length of red
yarn, embroider a ½ in
backstitch. Overstitch with
several small blanket stitches
and fasten off.

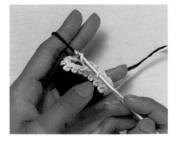

Bumblebees

Using black yarn and hook,
crochet two bumblebees as
follows:
1st–7th rows: work as 1st–7th
rows of ladybug.
8th–10th rows: change to
yellow yarn and work as 4th
row of ladybug.
11th–13th rows: change to

black yarn and work as 4th row of ladybug.

14th–16th rows: change to yellow yarn and work as 14th–16th rows of ladybug. Make eyes and mouth as for ladybug.

Wings

Using light blue yarn and hook, crochet two wings for each bee as follows:

3 ch, ss in first st to form a ring. 1 ch, into ring work 1 sc, 1 hdc, 4 dc, 1 hdc, 1 sc, ss in first ss, 2 ch. Cast off leaving 6–8 in of yarn to stitch the wings to the bee.

Flower

This is crocheted in two halves, one orange and one green. Using orange yarn and hook, crochet the flower as follows:

3 ch, ss in first st to form a ring.

1st row: 1 ch, 5 sc into ring, ss in first st at beginning of round.

2nd row: 1 ch, 2 sc in each of next 5 sts, ss in first st.

3rd row: 1 ch, 2 sc in each of next 10 sts, ss in first st.

4th row: 1 ch, * 1 sc in each of first 4 sts, 2 sc in next st. Repeat from * three more times, ss in first st.

5th row: 1 ch, * 1 sc in each

of first 5 sts, 2 sc in next st. Repeat from * three more times, ss in first st.

6th row: 1 ch, * 1 sc in each of first 6 sts, 2 sc in next st. Repeat from * three more times, ss in first st.

7th row: 1 ch, * 1 sc in each of first 6 sts, 2 sc in next st. Repeat from * three more times, ss in first st.

8th row: 1 ch, 1 sc in each of next 36 sts, ss in first st.

9th and 10th rows: repeat 8th row. Crochet a length of chain, long enough to hang the mobile, and cast off. Repeat 1st–10th rows in green yarn for the back half of the flower. On 10th row, do not make a chain as for the front, but leave 28 in of yarn to stitch the back and front halves together.

Petals

Using different colored yarns and hook, crochet nine petals as follows:

3 ch, ss in first st to form a ring.

1st row: 2 ch, 8 dc into ring, ss in first st at beginning of round.

2nd row: 2 ch, 1 sc in first st, 2 sc in first st, 2 sc in each of next 5 sts. Cast off leaving approximately a 16 in length of yarn to stitch the petal to the flower.

To make up

Stitch each petal to the orange half of the flower. Before fastening off each color, embroider several back stitches at the center of the flower. When all nine petals are attached, stitch the

green and orange halves of the flower together, stuffing loosely as you do so.

Bees and ladybugs gather around a bright summer flower. (Rachel Howard Marshall)

To assemble

Cut two pieces of jewelry wire, each measuring approximately 30 in. Bend one piece of wire in half and thread onto a large-eyed needle. Thread through the top of the green part of the flower ¾ in either side of the yellow hanging chain. Pull through the wire so there are

equal amounts of wire on either side of the flower. Thread one end of the wire through the top of a bee. Bend back the wire by ¾ in and twist. Thread a ladybug onto the other end of the wire in the same way. At the point where the wire joins the bee, cast on with needle and green yarn and blanket stitch along the wire to the flower. Thread the needle and yarn through the flower and continue to blanket stitch down the wire to the ladybug. Fasten off. Attach the second bee and ladybug to the bottom of the flower in the same way.

Butterflies

Decorated with vibrant felt
butterflies, this unusual coiled
mobile can be hung vertically
or suspended horizontally
above a cot or pram.

tools and materials

cardboard | 12 8 in × 8 in pieces of felt in assorted colors |
scissors | dressmaker's pins | fabric glue | needle and
thread | 8 × 16 in piece of black felt | thin jewelry
wire | wire cutters | 4 × 4 in piece of yellow felt |
63 × ¾ in strip of green felt | thick galvanized wire |
flat-nosed pliers | insulating tape | strong thread |

1 Trace and cut out separate templates for the butterfly wings, spots and body, using the template at the back of the book as a guide. Place two pieces of felt in contrasting colors one on top of the other. Pin the wing and both spot templates to the felt and cut out. Glue the felt spots to the wings, reversing the colors. Sew around the edges of the wings. Repeat with the remaining pieces of colored felt. Cut 12 body shapes from black felt. Glue a body piece in the center of one side of each of the wings. Cut six 14 in lengths of thin jewelry wire and bend them in half.

Bend back each end a little, so no sharp pieces of wire protrude.

For each pair of antennae, cut two strips of black felt 4 × ⅝ in. Fold each strip in half lengthwise and stitch ¼ in from the folded edge. Trim and slip onto the ends of the bent wire. Cut four yellow felt circles ½ in in diameter. Glue a yellow circle on either side of the antennae.

2 Position the antennae in the center of the wings and place a body piece over the exposed wire. Stitch all the way around the edges of the body.

3 Fold the strip of green felt in half lengthwise. Stitch ¼ in from the folded edge and trim. Cut a 65 in length of thick wire and feed through the green felt tube. Bend back both ends of the wire and bind with tape. Bend the covered wire into a large double coil. Firmly stitch a length of strong thread halfway along the wire's length for hanging.

4 Attach one butterfly to each end of the mobile by sewing a small rectangle of black felt to each butterfly's body. Sew around three sides of the rectangle, leaving the bottom end open. Insert one tape-bound wire end into each pocket and stitch in place. Sew the remaining four butterflies at equal distances from each other along the wire.

The green felt-covered wire spiral makes an unusual mobile frame, representing the stems of plants on which the butterflies rest. (Rachel Howard Marshall)

Lions

Made from soft felts in
sunshine colors, these funny lions
with moving eyes will appeal
to babies.

tools and materials

scissors | felt scraps | thin batting | needle and
thread | fabric glue | 10 moving eyes | black embroidery
thread | dressmaker's pins | 2 wooden rods | acrylic
paints | paintbrushes | wood glue | nylon thread |

*The bright colors and bold
shapes of these friendly
felt lions are reflected
in this mobile's cheerful
wooden crossbar.
(Dinah Alan-Smith)*

1 For each lion, cut out two bodies, manes and ears, and one face, nose and tail from the felt scraps, using the templates at the back of the book. Cut out one body from the batting. Sew the face and ears to one mane piece. Stick on the nose and eyes and embroider a mouth.

2 Sew the two pieces of body together with the batting sandwiched in between. Sew a vertical row of stitching at the bottom of the body to make two legs.

3 Pin a mane piece to each side of the body and sew around the edge. Leave the bottom of the mane unstitched. Glue on the tail. Make four more lions in the same way.

4 Paint the wooden rods in bright orange and yellow paint. Glue the rods together to make a crossbar. Sew a length of thread to each lion. Tie the lions to the ends of the crossbar.

Teddy bears in a row

Designed to be suspended horizontally across a crib or carriage, these cheeky teddy bears are strung together with pompoms.

tools and materials

felt scraps | scissors | pen | embroidery thread and needle | dressmaker's pins | batting | pompoms | threading elastic | large needle |

1 Using the template at the back of the book as a guide, cut out eight teddy bear shapes from four different colors of felt. Draw a smiling face on four teddy bear shapes and embroider the features. Leave the other four shapes plain, for the teddy bears' backs.

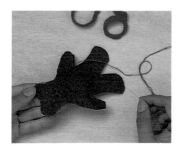

2 Pin together the teddy bear shapes in pairs and sew around the edges in running stitch. Leave a gap on one side for the batting.

3 Stuff the teddy bears and finish sewing around the edges.

4 With a large needle, thread the teddy bears and pompoms onto a length of elastic. Thread the teddy bears through the arms. Tie a loop at each end of the elastic for hanging the mobile.

These soft felt teddy bears on elastic will delight a baby. However, never leave your baby to play with a crib or carriage toy, such as this, unattended – even for a minute.
(Labeena Ishaque)

Flowers

Soft, brilliantly colored felts and simple eye-catching shapes make perfect mobiles for babies, encouraging them to focus and follow the gentle movement.

tools and materials

florist's wire | *wire cutters* | *strong tape* | *felt scraps* | *scissors* | *white glue* | *needle and embroidery thread* | *colored thread* | *brass ring* |

Opposite page:
Use up scraps of felt to create
a hanging garden of flowers,
whatever the time of year.
(Petra Boase)

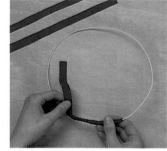

1 Cut a length of wire and curve into a ring. Secure the ends with strong tape.

2 Cover the ring in strips of felt. Glue in place and sew as necessary.

3 Cut out a variety of felt flowers in different colors, shapes and sizes. For each flower, build up layers of varied shapes and add a center in a contrasting color to each side. Sew a cross-stitch in the center of each flower to secure the pieces firmly.

4 Tie four colored threads to the wire ring, tie the ends together and sew on a brass ring for hanging. Cover the brass ring with a strip of felt. Sew threads onto the felt flowers and attach to the wire ring.

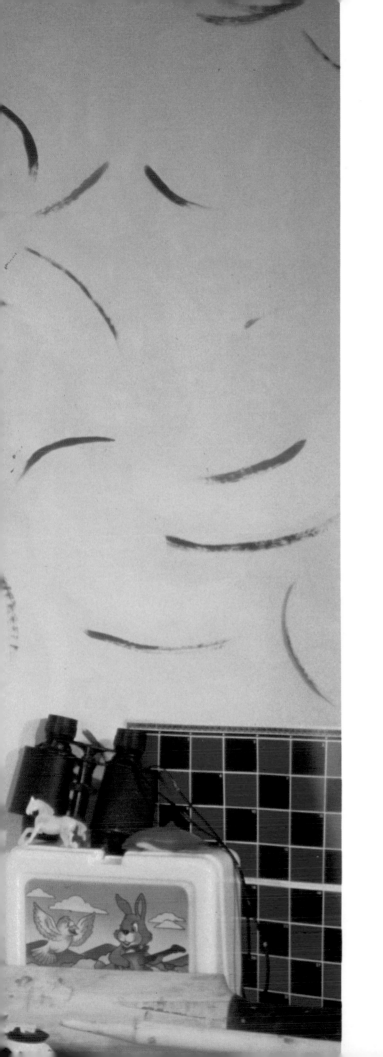

Child's play

mobiles for children

Mobiles are obvious decorations for a child's bedroom and can be made or chosen to add a vivid flash of color at ceiling height. They are especially popular if they include images of a child's favorite hobbies and pastimes, be it circus elephants, farm animals or a delightful peg doll family. Children will also love to help make any of these fun mobiles.

Artists' gallery

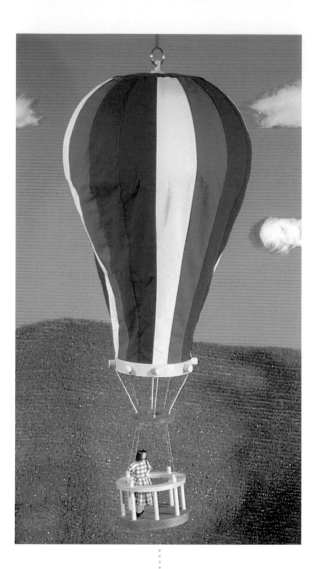

Up and away

*Objects which fly or float
have always provided inspiration
for mobiles. This hot-air
balloon evokes the boundless
reaches of the sky.
(Checkpoint)*

Trapeze artist

*Mobiles needn't always have
more than one hanging element.
The clown is attached to the
trapeze by elastic so that he jumps
when the mobile is moved.
(Checkpoint)*

Parrot fashion

*Three-dimensional parrots sit
realistically on bamboo perches,
one above the other.
(7 & 7 Interiors)*

Cast a spell

*The benign wizard and his host
of familiars hang beneath a vibrant
magical flash.
(Jim Edminston/Lucky Parrot)*

Instant inspiration

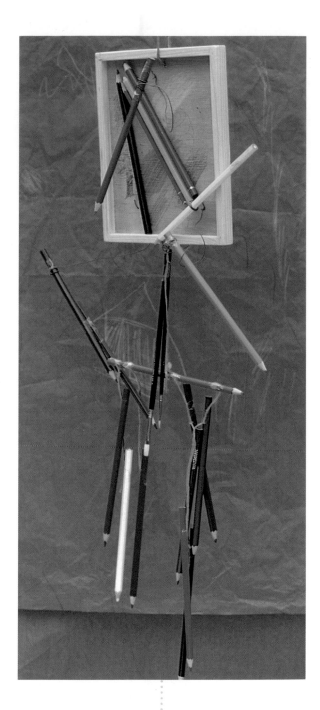

Plane fun

*Hang model airplanes
from kebab sticks for the child who
dreams of flying.*

Pencils

*For budding young artists,
hang pencils from a small wooden
picture frame. The clean lines
of the pencils and the angles they
create are very pleasing to the eye.*

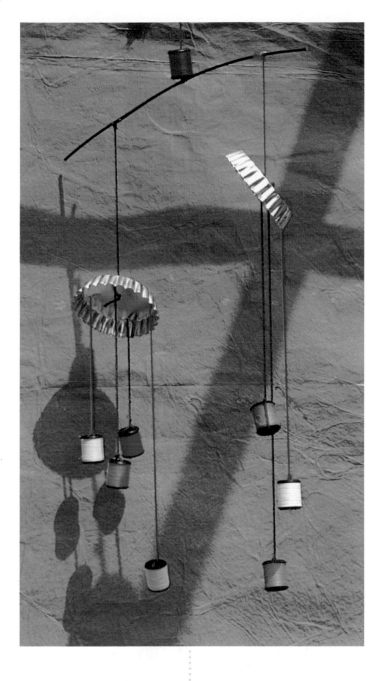

Colored spools

*Tie miniature cotton reels
with brightly colored thread
around the edges of metallic
cupcake cases and hang the
clusters from a central bar, for a
creative child.*

Parasols

*Cocktail umbrellas, perhaps
collected by your child when on
vacation, can be suspended
one above the other to make a
delicate and amusing mobile.*

Peg doll family

This exquisite family of
peg dolls is suspended from an
outsize wooden peg, made
from a piece of dowelling or a
broom handle.

tools and materials

piece of broom handle or dowelling of a similar size |
sandpaper | *coping saw* | *drill* | *4 dolly pegs* |
small wooden knob | *craft knife* | *pipe cleaners* |
fabric scraps | *white glue* | *needle and thread* |
black and white marker pens | *embroidery thread* |
small hooks | *fine cord* |

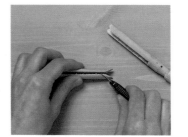

1 Sand down the piece of
broom handle or
dowelling. Saw a curved slit
in one end of the dowelling at
an angle to make a peg
shape. If you are not
confident about doing this,
ask for the slit to be cut when
you buy the dowelling.

2 Drill four holes along
the dowelling. Drill a
hole towards the top of each
dolly peg. Glue the wooden
knob onto the other end of
the dowelling to make a
giant peg.

3 Cut off the ends of two
of the dolly pegs at an
angle, to make the shorter
children.

4 Push a pipe cleaner
through the hole drilled
in each dolly peg. Fold over
the ends by ¼ in to make
hands.

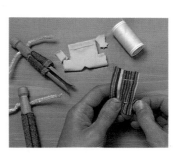

5 To make pants and
shorts, glue a rectangle
of fabric around each peg leg
and hide the seams between
the legs.

6 Make a T-shirt by
cutting two "T" shapes
from fabric. Turn up a hem at
the bottom and sew the side
and sleeve seams. Make a
shirt in the same way. Make
skirts and bodices for the
other two peg dolls.

7 Draw faces and shoes
on all the dolls and hair
on the man and boy. Glue
embroidery thread for hair on
the woman and girl.

8 Screw a hook into each doll's head. Tie fine cord to each of the dolls and thread these through the holes in the big peg and knot to secure. Take a longer length of fine cord and thread the ends through the outer holes in the big peg. Adjust the length, knot firmly and use for hanging the mobile.

Traditional peg dolls are here displayed as a family and make a charming decoration for a little girl's bedroom.
(Dorothy Wood)

Counting sheep

A mobile for parents to give their children to help them sleep! Pompom sheep have their own twiggy fences to jump over.

tools and materials

cardboard | *scissors* | *cream wool* | *pipe cleaners* | *brown felt scraps* | *white glue* | *dark brown thread* | *twigs* | *ribbon* |

1 To make a pompom, cut out two doughnut-shaped pieces of cardboard. Place the pieces of cardboard together and wind cream wool around the cardboard until the ring is filled. Cut through the wool around the edge with a pair of sharp scissors. Tightly tie a short length of wool between the two pieces of cardboard. Remove the cardboard and fluff out the pompom. Make three pompoms in this way.

2 To make the legs, push two pipe cleaners through each pompom. Bend up the ends to make four feet.

3 To make the faces, cut out four semicircles of dark brown felt and roll into tight cones. Glue the edges and glue the faces onto the pompom sheep.

4 With dark brown thread, bind together small pieces of twig to make miniature fences. Make two fences in this way.

5 Cut a groove at the center of two larger twigs and glue together. Bind the join with thread. For a larger mobile, use three twigs and make extra pompom sheep and fences.

6 Tie the sheep and fences to the twig crosspiece, adjusting the threads until you achieve the right balance. Tie a ribbon to the center of the crosspiece for hanging.

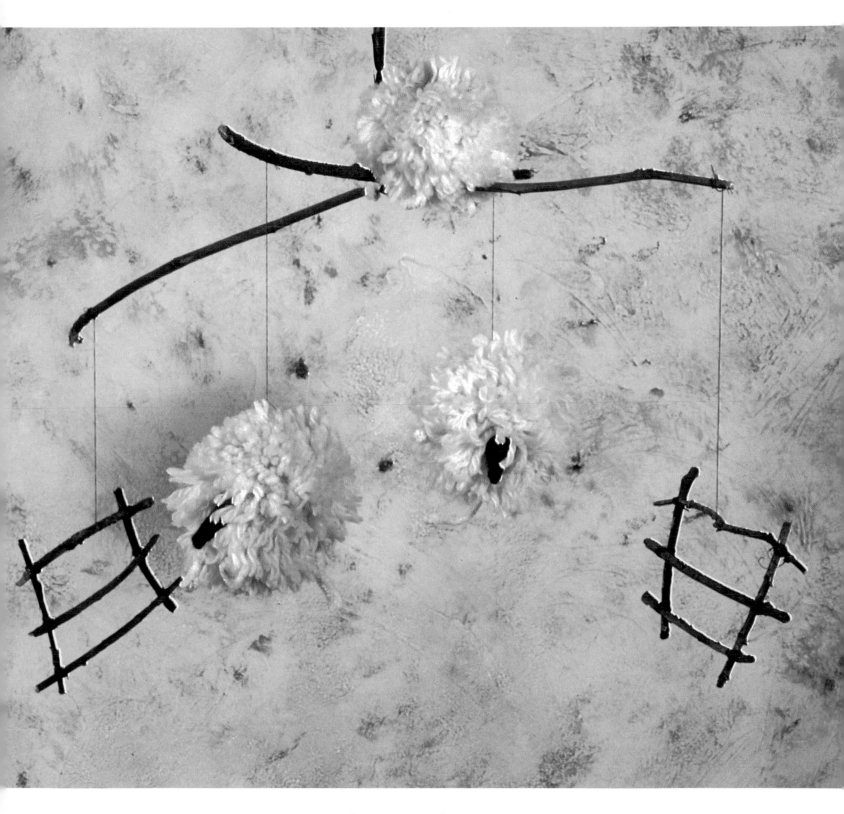

Pompoms are great fun to
make and are here transformed into
sheep by the addition of pipe
cleaner legs and felt noses.
(Labeena Ishaque)

Glitter ornaments

This sparkly mobile is made using paper balls decorated with glitter, foil shapes, colored pipe cleaners and glass gems – great fun for a child to make at home.

tools and materials

florist's wire | *scissors* | *sticky-backed felt* | *paper balls* | *poster paints* | *paintbrushes* | *glitter* | *colored pipe cleaners* | *sequins* | *glass gems* | *colored foil shapes* | *white glue* | *gold and silver elastic thread* | *needle* | *fine silver cord* |

Use whatever you have to hand to decorate these fun paper ornaments – children will love to try it. (Petra Boase)

1 Curve a length of florist's wire and twist the ends together to make a ring. Wrap strips of sticky-backed felt around the wire ring.

2 Paint the balls with poster paints and allow to dry. Decorate the balls with the glitter, coiled pipe cleaners, sequins, gems and colored foil shapes, using white glue to attach them.

3 Make a small ring from florist's wire, wrap with sticky-backed felt and attach it to one of the balls with four short lengths of gold and silver elastic thread. Tie four pieces of elastic thread to the large ring and sew the ends to the central ball.

4 Thread a length of fine silver cord through each ball and knot firmly to secure. Tie the other ends to the large ring.

Farm animals

This sweet mobile is made from salt dough. Try to make the animals the same size, or in pairs, so they will balance easily.

tools and materials

2 cups flour | 1 cup salt | 1 cup water | rolling pin | animal cutters | paper clips | scissors | waxed paper | baking tray | craft paints | paintbrushes | matte varnish | 2 wooden dowels | drill | white glue | wood stain | raffia | 2 large wooden beads |

1 Make a salt dough using the flour, salt and water. Knead thoroughly. Roll out to a thickness of ⅓ in. Cut out the animals. Smooth the edges with a wet finger. Cut the paper clips in half and press a half into the back of each animal to form a loop for hanging.

2 Bake the animals in an oven at 250°F for about 8 hours or until the dough has completely dried. Paint the animals, using a dry brush for a stippled effect. Apply three coats of matte varnish and allow to dry.

3 Drill four evenly spaced holes along each dowel, and glue together to form a cross. Drill a hole through the join and paint the crosspiece with wood stain.

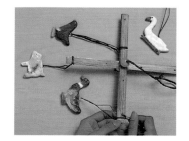

4 Tie each animal to the crosspiece with raffia. Thread a raffia loop through the crosspiece's center, securing on either side with a wooden bead.

Animal-shaped pastry cutters are used to cut the animal shapes from salt dough. Vary the theme using wild animal or sea creature cutters, if desired.
(Lucinda Ganderton)

Elephants

The circus comes to town with these beautiful miniature felt elephants suspended from a painted podium.

tools and materials

round plastic container | acrylic gesso | paintbrushes | poster paints | fine gold braid and thread | white glue | felt | tailor's chalk | scissors | sequins and beads | needle and thread | batting | awl |

1 Paint the container in several coats of acrylic gesso. Allow to dry. Draw triangles around the side and paint with lilac, purple and pink poster paints.

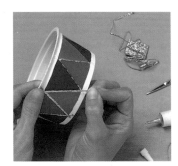

2 Glue strips of gold braid along the diagonal lines between the colored triangles.

3 Use the template at the back of the book to draw pairs of elephant outlines on the felt, using tailor's chalk. Cut out two ears for each elephant.

4 Before cutting out the felt elephants, sew on braid and sequins to make gaily-colored rugs on the elephants' backs. Sew on beads for the eyes and embroider chainstitch on the ankles, using the gold thread.

5 Cut out the elephants and sew each pair together around the edges, leaving a gap for batting. Stuff the elephants, using a skewer to fill the trunks. Close up the gap by oversewing. Sew on the ears and gold threads for the tails.

6 Sew a length of fine gold thread onto the back of each elephant for hanging them.

7 Make a hole for each elephant to hang from in the rim of the container, spacing them equally, and one in the center of the base, using an awl or other pointed implement. Hang the elephants and add a thread at the top for hanging.

Simple felt elephants are decorated with sequins and braid to represent the rich tapestry of Indian blankets.
(Dorothy Wood)

Templates

Templates are guides which can be traced around in order to transfer an outline or a design onto the material from which an object is made. All these templates need to be enlarged to bring them up to the actual size of the original designs. You can do this by enlarging them on a photocopier so that each square measures ⅝ in. To enlarge using the grid method, draw a larger grid with each square measuring ⅝ in onto a sheet of tracing paper. Copy the template taking each square individually and drawing the relevant part of the outline in the larger square. Finally, draw over the lines to make sure they are continuous and easy to trace.

Mobile phones p59

×2

×2

Christmas cans p43

Tin can template
(adapt and repeat as required)

Tin shape templates

Abstract face 2 p70/71

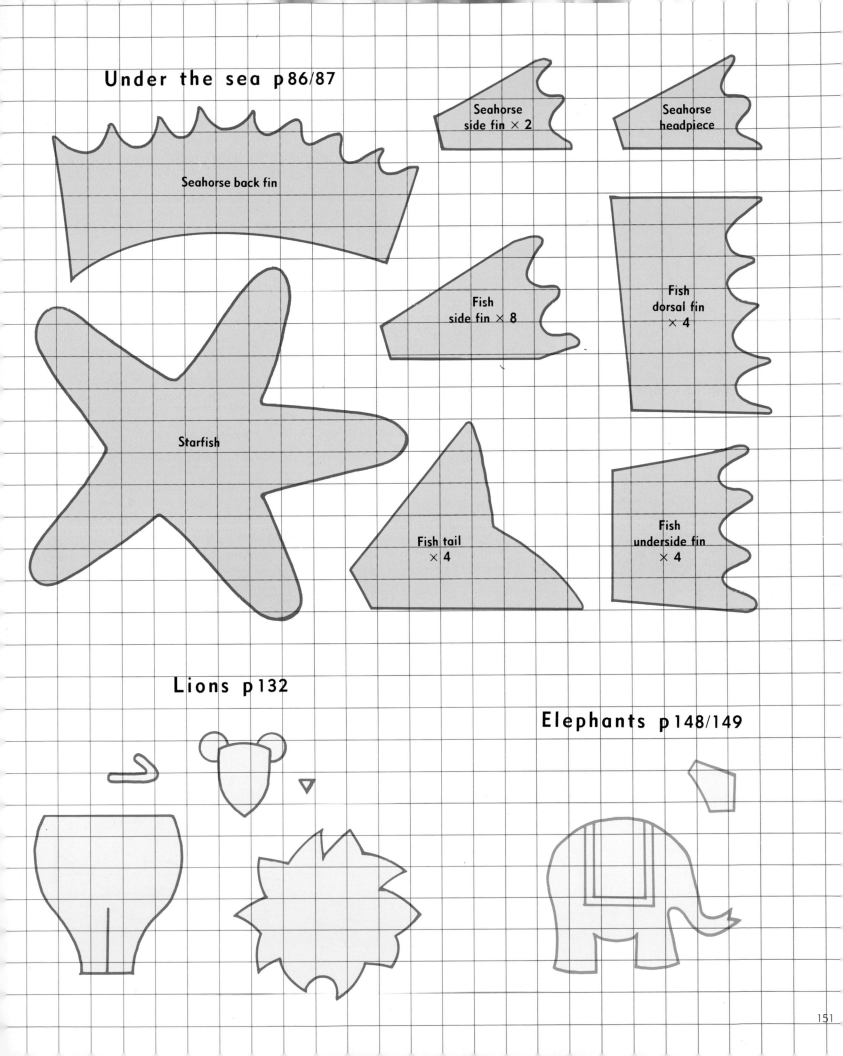

Under the sea p86/87

Seahorse back fin

Seahorse side fin × 2

Seahorse headpiece

Starfish

Fish side fin × 8

Fish dorsal fin × 4

Fish tail × 4

Fish underside fin × 4

Lions p132

Elephants p148/149

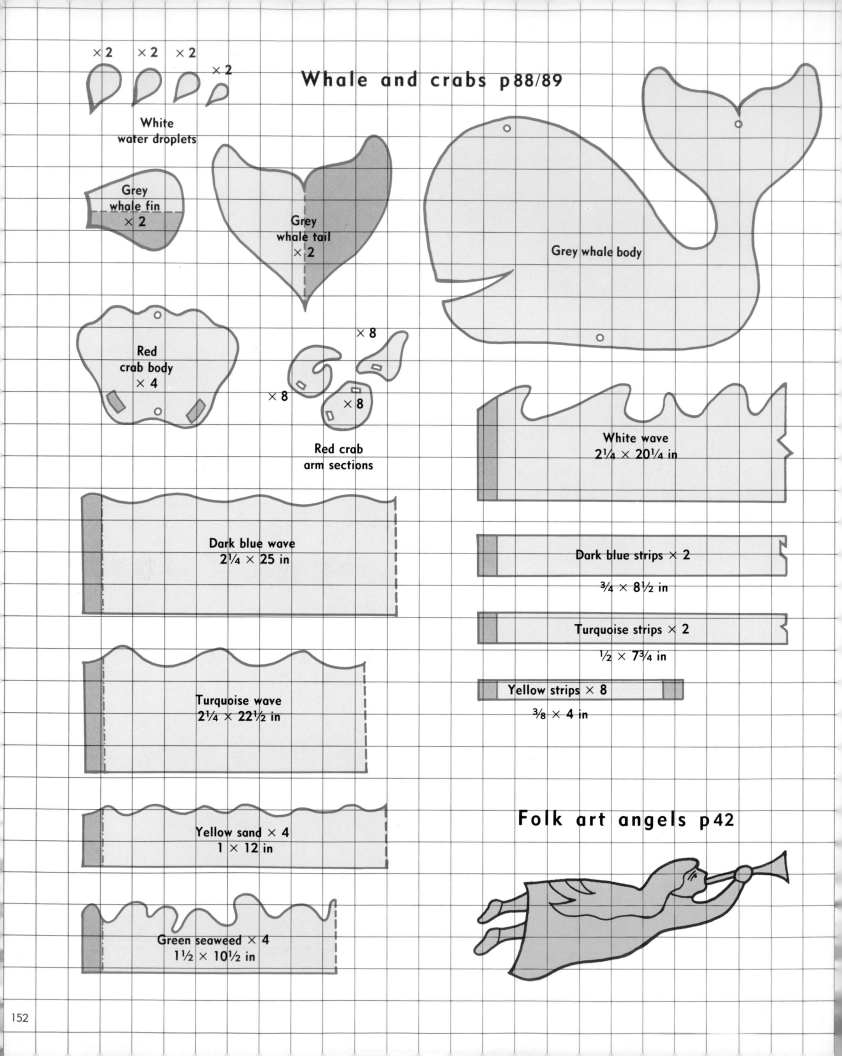

×2 ×2 ×2
×2

White
water droplets

Whale and crabs p88/89

Grey
whale fin
× 2

Grey
whale tail
× 2

Grey whale body

Red
crab body
× 4

× 8

× 8

× 8

Red crab
arm sections

White wave
2¼ × 20¼ in

Dark blue wave
2¼ × 25 in

Dark blue strips × 2

¾ × 8½ in

Turquoise strips × 2

½ × 7¾ in

Turquoise wave
2¼ × 22½ in

Yellow strips × 8

⅜ × 4 in

Yellow sand × 4
1 × 12 in

Folk art angels p42

Green seaweed × 4
1½ × 10½ in

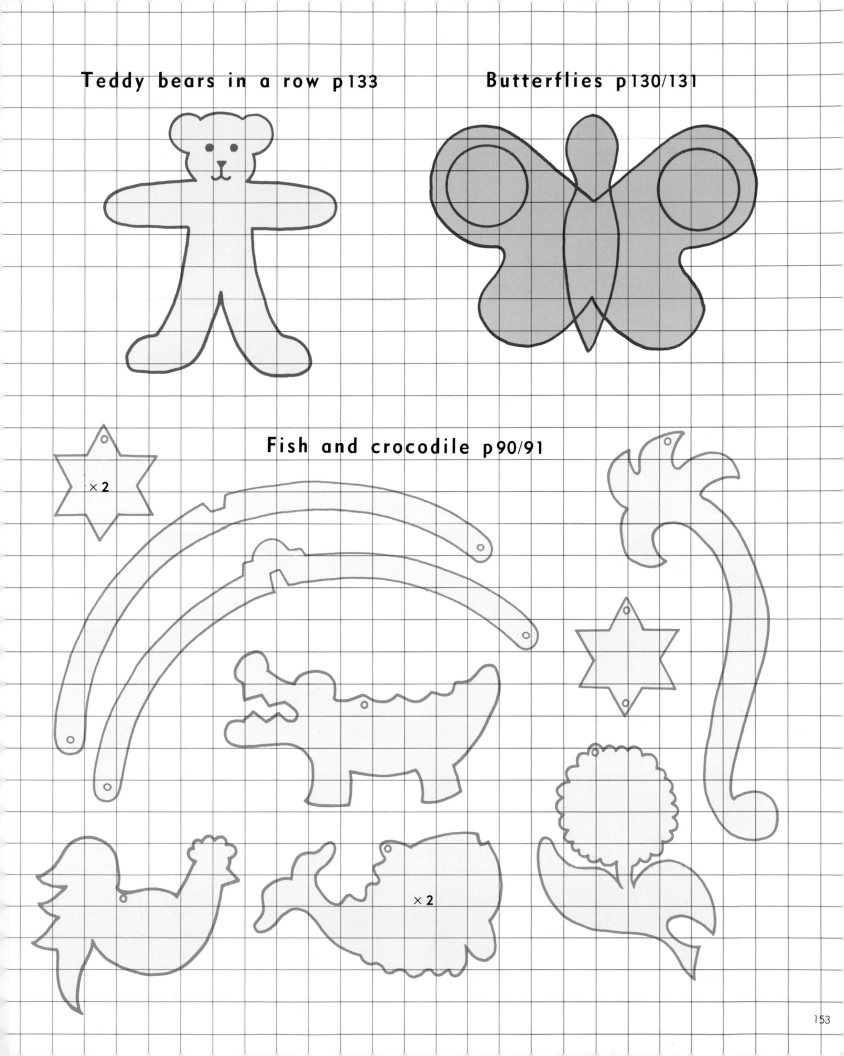

Teddy bears in a row p133

Butterflies p130/131

Fish and crocodile p90/91

×2

×2

153

Bird watching p 56/57

× 3

× 2

×2

×2

×5

Sealed with a kiss p116

×2

×2

Abstract face 1 p69

Teatime p104/105

Octopus's garden p84/85

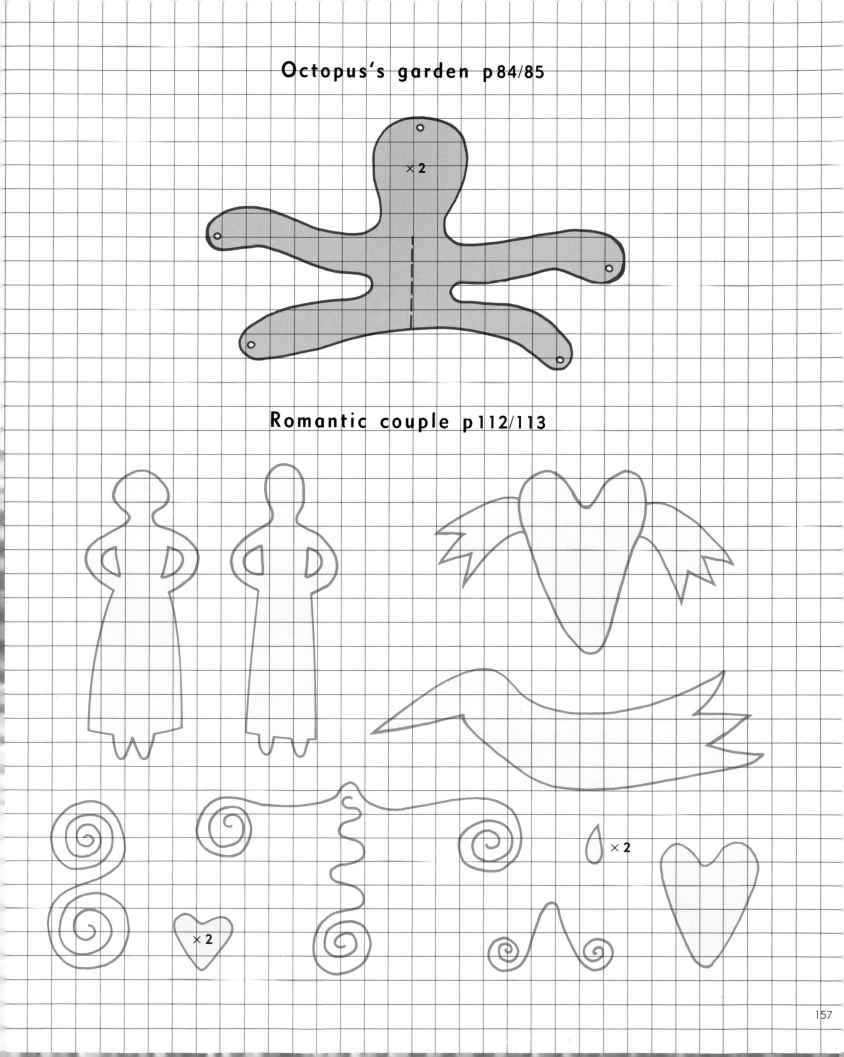

Romantic couple p112/113

×2

×2

×2

Index

Suppliers

Arts supplies

All Craft Tool and Supply
Company, Inc.
3rd Floor
45 West 46th Street
New York 11217

Art Supply Warehouse
360 Main Avenue
Norwalk
Connecticut 06851

Kate's Paperie
8 West 13th Street
New York
New York 10001

Papersource Inc
730 N Franklin Suite 111
Chicago
Illinois 60610

Daniel Smith, Inc.
Fine Artists Materials
4130 First Avenue South
Seattle
Washington 98132

Decoupage supplies

Dover Publications Inc
31 East 2nd Street
Mineola
New York 11501
(212) 255 3755

Fabrics and sewing

DMC Corporation
Port Kearny
Building 10
South Kearny
New Jersey 07032
(threads and cottons)

P & B Fabrics
898 Mahler Road
Burlingame
California 94010

Jewelry supplies

Beads Galore International, Inc.
2123 South Priest
Suite #201
Tempe
Arizona 85282

The Clay Factory
PO Box 460598
Escondido
California 92046-0598
(tools, wires, modeling clay)

Handy and Harman
250 Park Avenue
New York 10017
(precious metals)

Yarn supplies

Christa's Ball & Skein
971 Lexington Avenue No.1A
New York
New York 10021
(212) 772 6960

Greenwich Yarns
2073 Greenwich Street
San Francisco 94123
(415) 567 2535

Hook 'N' Needle
1869 Post Road East
Westport
Connecticut 06880
(203) 259 5119

Mixed Media
2531 Rocky Ridge Road No.101
Birmingham
Alabama 35243
(205) 822 5855

Straw Into Gold
3006 San Pablo Avenue
Berkeley
California 94702

Contributors

The author and publishers
would like to thank the
following people for producing
the wonderful mobiles
specially created for this book:

Ofer Acoo, Dinah Alan-Smith,
Deborah Alexander, Michael
Ball, Petra Boase, Janet Bridge,
Al Brown, Lucinda Ganderton,
Lisa Gilchrist, Jill Hancock,
Bridget Hinge, Rachel Howard
Marshall, Labeena Ishaque,
Sameena Ishaque, Paul
Jackson, Kim Rowley, Debbie
Siniska, Thomasina Smith
(creator of the Instant
Inspiration mobiles), Karen
Triffitt, Josephine Whitfield,
Melanie Williams, and
Dorothy Wood.

Artists' gallery

The author and publishers
gratefully acknowledge the
following individuals and
companies who loaned mobiles
for the gallery sections:

7 & 7 Interiors
Checkpoint
James Dean
Sara Drake
The Lucky Parrot
Papier Marché
People and Planet
Pixi UK
Shaker
Louise Slater
Heidi Westgate
Mrs Winter

Credits

The author would like to thank
Labeena Ishaque, her assistant,
for being a wonderful hand
model and creative brain.

The author and publishers
would like to thank the
following suppliers for loaning
materials and equipment:

Fred Aldous Limited
Creative Beadcraft
Inscribe
Lead and Light